SUPERTIMING

THE UNIQUE ELLIOTT WAVE SYSTEM

KEYS TO ANTICIPATING IMPENDING STOCK MARKET ACTION

BY
ROBERT C. BECKMAN

HARRIMAN HOUSE LTD

3A Penns Road
Petersfield
Hampshire
GU32 2EW
GREAT BRITAIN

Tel: +44 (0)1730 233870
Email: enquiries@harriman-house.com
Website: www.harriman-house.com

First edition published in the United States of America by The Library of Investment Study in 1979.
This second edition published by Harriman House in 2014.

ISBN: 978-0-85719-340-7

British Library Cataloguing in Publication Data
A CIP catalogue record for this book can be obtained from the British Library.

FOLLOW US, LIKE US, EMAIL US

@HarrimanHouse

www.linkedin.com/company/harriman-house

www.facebook.com/harrimanhouse

contact@harriman-house.com

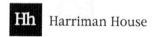

Contents

Publisher's Preface, 1979   vii

Introduction   xi

One: The Origins of the Wave Principle   1

First contacts with Wall Street   2

Elliott and the Economists   5

The Grand Super Cycle   6

The Five-wave Concept   7

The Need to be a Genius?   10

Two: Reality in the Stock Market   11

$2,000 to $1,000,000   12

The Future not the Past   13

Cyclical Nature of the Market   16

Time Frame Relative – not Fixed   20

Classification of Waves   22

Three: Elliott... Pure and Simple   27

A Rhythmic Pattern of Waves   28

Elliott's Five Basic Tenets   29

Bull Market – Bear Market   30

Ground Rules   32

Application to Investment Strategy   34

Probabilities not Absolutes   35

Practice Runs   36

Four: "Like a Circle in a Spiral, a Wheel within a Wheel"   39

The Wave Count   40

Breakdown of Primary Market Cycle   42

Pivotal Points   44

1984?   45

Normality and Variations   46

The Market is Always Right   48

Improving Investment Performance   48

Five: The Fibonacci Summation Series   **51**

The Series   52

W. D. Gann's Numerical Approach   54

The Fibonacci Series in Art and Nature   55

Examples from *Nature's Law*   57

Fibonacci and Cyclical Behaviour   58

Brilliant... or Ludicrous?   58

Open Mind – Successful Investment   60

Six: Applying the Fibonacci Series   **61**

Choice of Stock Exchange Data   62

A Psychological Phenomenon   64

Pattern   65

Time   68

Ratio   71

Calculations and Examples   72

The "Non-Absolute" Nature of Elliott   74

Stock Market History and the Summation Series   75

Seven: The Trend Channel   **77**

Logarithmic and Arithmetic Scales   79

Forecasting using Trend Channels   80

Frames of Reference, not Predictions   84

Deviations from "Normative" Behaviour   85

F.T.30, January 1975-February 1976   87

Eight: Elliott, Inflation and the Fifth Wave   **91**

Inflation in Britain   92

Inflation in the U.S.A. and Fibonacci   93

Early Warnings of Inflation   95

Extensions   96

Extensions of Extensions   100

Retracements and Double Retracements   101

Double Retracement and the Extended Fifth Wave   103

Nine: Incorrigible Behaviour   **107**

Extensions in the Corrective Phase   109

Corrective Wave Formations – "Zigzag"   110

Maximum Corrective Action   112

Use in Investment Strategy   115

Further Corrective Wave Formations   117

The "Flat"   118

"Irregular Corrections"   122

**Ten: "Double Threes", "Triple Threes",
"Horizontals", "Triangles"… and all that!**   **127**

Complex Corrections   129

Triangles and Horizontals   133

The Tension in the Triangle   141

Enlargement of Corrections   143

Use of the Time Factor   145

Action after the Corrective Wave   146

Eleven: The Finishing Touches   **149**

Breakdown of the Impulse Waves   151

Elliott's Theory of Alternation   153

Erroneous Counting   156

"Failures"   159

"Thrusts"   161
Volume   162
Moving Averages   165
Ancillary Indicators   169

Twelve: Practical Application of the Wave Principle   171
Terminal Endings   173
The Next Ten Years   175
Sequence for Selling   177
Trading Intermediate Term Movements   179
Confirmation of Terminal Junctures   181
Applications to Individual Share Price Movements   183
The Final Word   185

Appendix: "The Wave Principle"   187
Introducing "The Wave Principle"   188
The Wave Principle: Part II   191
The Wave Principle: Part III   194
The Wave Principle: Part IV   197
The Wave Principle: Part V   199
The Wave Principle: Part VI   203
The Wave Principle: Part VII   205
The Wave Principle: Part VIII   208
The Wave Principle: Part IX   211
The Wave Principle: Part X   214
The Wave Principle: Part XI   218
The Wave Principle: Part XII   220

Bibliography   223

Publisher's Preface, 1979

(Some very important notes)

IN PUBLISHING THIS far-reaching book on the Elliott Wave Principle, material which has for too long laid undeservedly neglected, it is hoped that we will have helped in opening new vistas to the study of market timing. And further to this book, at the end of this Preface, we offer a way that some readers will want to pursue in looking for a deeper enlightenment in the unique approach of R.N. Elliott, and possibly other approaches, to the continuing analysis of the action in the trading marketplaces.

Having been associated with the Author for a number of years, we can attest to the high place he holds in our esteem in his knowledge and utilization of the Elliott Wave theory in actual investment practice. And especially in the light of the contents of this book, we feel that a few additional words about the Author will help in the enjoyment and understanding of this work. Following several years of active involvement in the investment field on Wall Street, leaving his native land he settled in London, England where he saw a great opportunity in the various fields of finance. Just a few years later he was instrumental in starting the prestigious Investors Bulletin, a weekly advisory service to British investors and institutions, in which he continues to apply his American market knowledge and training to analysing the movement of shares on the London Stock Exchange.

With an intimate knowledge of both New York and London markets and with both rich in their own historical movements, it was only natural that he would draw from both in presenting examples of

Elliott's precepts. The major part of this work was originally written in 1976 by Mr. Beckman for his British audience where he is very well known from his daily radio broadcasts of market analysis and opinions. Naturally, some British references and examples were included for this audience, and in adapting the work for its American publication some were removed and others have been left as originally set forth since they certainly have something to add to their own knowledge of financial conditions in other parts of the world.

Taking the past 10 years as a single period, and comparing movements of the major stock exchanges around the world, the London market has undoubtedly been the most dynamic in its swings in plunging to extreme major lows and rising to all-time highs. This alone makes it a splendid market to use for good examples of Elliott's wave system, and for readers mainly familiar with only moves of the New York Stock Exchange and the Dow-Jones 30, the experience of seeing the detailed action of another very important market should prove equally rewarding.

From time to time Mr. Beckman also makes reference to some of the broad movements in London over this 10 year span of time and to help in following these references we have added the chart on the following page. This graph shows the monthly movement of the London F.T.30 Index, or to give its full and proper title – the Financial Times Ordinary Share Index. This is the direct and comparable equivalent of our own Dow-Jones 30 Index. Turning to this particular chart when Mr. Beckman discusses some of the historical movements of this Index will give the reader the perspective to follow the points he makes.

To clear up a term that will be found to be unfamiliar when first seeing it, on the chart found on page 14, which shows the daily action of the F.T.30 over the stated period, the words "Bargains total" can be seen. In London this is the measurement of the daily volume, and it is actually the volume as measured by each reported dealing in each company's shares. One Bargain represents one trade whether it is for 10, 100 or 1,000, or whatever number of shares. Another fact that should be noted is that the F.T.30 is only compiled and reported once an hour and at the close of trading each day as compared to the D.J.30 where we have minute to minute reporting.

FINANCIAL TIMES ORDINARY SHARE INDEX (F.T.30)

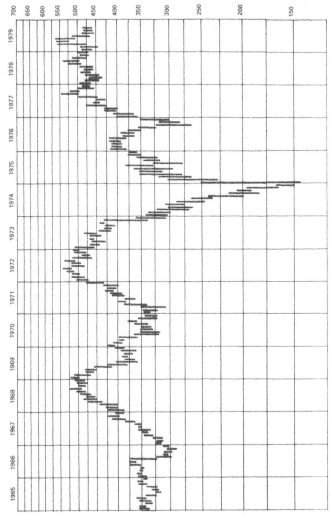

Financial Times Ordinary Share Index
(F.T. 30)

Throughout the text of this book can be found slight differences in the spelling of several words, and these reflect the small variations in the two usages of the English language in each country. As these differences are so few and so slight, we have left them as they were originally set out to avoid giving any added confusion to our typesetters. We doubt that they will prove of any bother to the reader.

Introduction

DURING AN ILLNESS in the mid-1930's, the late R.N. Elliott undertook the painstaking procedure of attempting to classify share price movements for the preceding 80 years on Wall Street. It was during the course of this work that Elliott discovered a definable basic rhythm in share price movements which he felt had forecasting value when correctly applied. In 1938 Elliott published his findings in a monograph entitled "The Wave Principle". Eight years later, as a result of further discoveries, he updated the original work in another thesis entitled "Nature's Law". Since then, with the exception of a few notable analysts who have achieved outstanding success with Elliott's theory, the work has drifted into relative obscurity, both of these works being long out of print while the only practitioners of the Elliott Wave Principle are now in North America.

The Elliott Wave theory will probably never achieve the acclaim it deserves for many reasons. Firstly, it is somewhat of a hybrid theory. It belongs in the category of those tools which attempt to analyse the stock market on technical grounds yet is anathema to most "chartists" who only have confidence in "trend chasing" methods. In addition, the Elliott Wave principle makes no claim to predict the future, although far more startling results have been achieved with Elliott than with certain popular methods which do make such claims. Probably the most severe impediment to the popularity of the method is the initial apparent complexity and variations that must be recognised. The technical methods of dealing with share price movements that have gained popularity usually rely upon a mechanical approach which gives definite buy, sell or hold "signals", the technique of which can be mastered in a few short hours. I warn you, this is not the case with the "Wave Principle". Mastery of this technique will take a great deal of time and patience and judgement in its application. Furthermore, before one can apply the principle with sufficient confidence to make it a profitable experience, most conventional stock market theory will have to be placed in "suspense" in the recognition that the stock market offers no absolutes and there is no man alive who can predict with any useful, meaningful degree of accuracy where share prices will be one day hence, much less one year or more hence.

The far-sighted investor who has recognised the basic weakness in the many analytical approaches to the stock market will find the "Wave Principle" intellectually appealing. He will recognise the fact that although the probabilities governing share price behaviour may be 100:1 in his favour, there is always that "1". He will neither be intimidated nor dismayed by the emergence of the improbable as he watches the varying possibilities and probabilities unfold in the Wave Principle, and will incorporate the results in an investment strategy geared to his own personal requirements. He will not use the Wave Principle as a substitute for thought but will allow the theory to provide the information necessary to quantify the probability of risk or reward in the stock market at any given time.

The Wave Principle will not be used to forecast or predict, but rather to establish targets of probable achievement within the context of broad market movements. The targets will not be absolute targets but will vary in accordance with the changing cyclical pattern of both the economy and the stock market. The Wave Principle will adjust itself to compensate for the unforeseen fundamental developments which are so often the nemesis of technical analysts, producing those treacherous "false signals". The Wave Principle is the only stock market tool that has ever been devised to compensate for alterations in fundamental conditions.

In many cases, investors have learned to distrust the information and opinions of popularly expressed stock market forecasts, for in the final analysis it has become nothing more than a matter of how long the forecaster will be right before he is ruefully wrong. The "Wave Principle" provides an entirely new approach to this problem. Conceptually, the words "right" or "wrong" should now be eliminated from the approach to stock market price movements. A study of the

Wave Principle will train one to recognise the occurrence of the improbable and its frequency. On the odd occasion, the improbable and the losses that result are completely unavoidable. However, one will witness the self-adjusting mechanism of the Wave Principle realising that any losses that occur as a result of the improbable will be more than compensated for, provided the correct compensatory action is always taken.

The Wave Principle will discipline its user to anticipate rather than follow. A return to the grass roots philosophy of "Buy Low and Sell High" will be the credo of the investor who studies the Wave Principle, allowing him to act independently of the emotionally driven stock market players who habitually buy too late and sell too late. The concept that one should "Buy High and Sell Higher" has long been refuted by the many studies of the academicians.

In 1938 *Financial World* printed a series of articles written by R.N. Elliott entitled "The Wave Principle". I have chosen these articles as offering the most suitable guide for studying Elliott's theory. Of great interest should be the "Publishers' Note" which states:

> "During the past seven or eight years. Publishers of financial magazines and organizations in the investment advisory field have been virtually flooded with 'systems' for which their proponents have claimed great accuracy in forecasting stock market movements. Some of them appeared to work for a while. It was immediately obvious that others had no value whatever. All have been looked upon by THE FINANCIAL WORLD with great scepticism. But after investigation of Mr. R.N. Elliott's Wave Principle THE FINANCIAL WORLD became convinced that a series of articles on this subject would be interesting and instructive to its readers. To the individual reader is left the determination of the value of the Wave Principle as a working tool in market forecasting, but it is believed that it should prove at least a useful check upon conclusions based on economic considerations."

The Editors

These articles comprise the appendix to this book and it is recommended that the student review the basic Elliott principles as outlined before commencing with the text. The object of my text is threefold. In reviewing the original work by Elliott one will find many "grey" areas which require further elucidation while several of the tenets will appear somewhat vague in terms of practical application. It will be the function of this work to focus on the various obscurities in an attempt to devise a workable format which in turn can be incorporated into an overall investment strategy. In addition, there are a few modifications to the theory which will be necessary in order to apply the method to share price movements on the London Stock Exchange. This will be accomplished by incorporating the work of several other analysts who have made observations on the Elliott Wave theory and have used it successfully. Finally, and probably most important, if one is to work with this tool and achieve maximum benefit one must adopt the correct conceptual approach and be sufficiently conversant with the rationale of the method so that one can act with confidence and consistency. For this purpose an entire chapter has been devoted to the empirical record of achievement by those who have used the Elliott Wave Principle in both London and Wall Street. In addition an extensive bibliography has been included for those who would like to undertake further investigation into the rationale behind the method.

During the post-war era there has been a great deal of complacency in the securities industry. Because the business cycle and the stock market cycle have been in a major cyclical upward trend, offering only shallow corrections, there seem to be many people, even with the securities industry itself, who have blinded themselves to the historical precedents of share price behaviour. Up until 1973, the post-war procedures were working well for the newcomers while many of the old-timers had been annihilated by previous market catastrophes. With the advert of the cyclical collapse in share prices between 1973-4 many analysts discovered to their dismay that the rules of the post-war era were just as useless as those which had been discarded previously. To those who still say "times have changed", that the old rules of the 1930's and 1940's no longer apply, and that any attempt to predict the future collapse of the economy and the stock market from the long term cyclical precedent is the height of folly, there is very little useful that can be said.

For those, however, who are willing to approach the subject of stock market behaviour with an open mind, who have faith in the fundamental laws of economics and the consistency of human nature, who would like to avoid the pitfalls that have deluded the investment community for decades, who wish to learn how to read the message of the stock market in its entirety, for those investors and analysts the Wave Principle is resurrected, and the precept, explanations, experiences, and observations are disclosed, in the hope that their study will prove financially rewarding as well as the most fascinating method of stock market analysis that they have ever encountered.

R. C. Beckman

One:

The Origins of the Wave Principle

"More zeal and energy, more fanatical hope, and more intense anguish have been expended over the past century in efforts to 'forecast' the stock market than in almost any other single line of human action."

Richard Dana Skinner

VERY LITTLE LITERATURE is currently available on the Elliott Wave Principle; Elliott died in 1948 and his monographs and "educational letters" have been out of print for decades. This factor alone will make this work all the more valuable to those interested in this highly intriguing theory of cyclical movements in the stock market.

While it is difficult to obtain the original work carried out by R. N. Elliott, his background and emergence into the securities industry would appear to be even more obscure. The late A. Hamilton Bond, president of Bolton, Tremblay & Company, and probably the world's principal exponent of Elliott's work had very little information to provide about Elliott the man, and in fact was never closely associated with him. In 1953, Bolton decided to publish a small pamphlet on what he thought the Elliott Wave Principle was saying about the U.S. stock market at that time. This was the first widely recognised publication of any material on Elliott since his death in 1948. For some reason none of Elliott's students had seen fit to carry on his work. Bolton had become intrigued with the possibilities of the Wave Principle when he first discovered the series of articles authored by Elliott in *The Financial World, circa* 1938. Following Elliott's death in 1948, only one or two students were willing to discuss the Wave Principle in any way. In his work, "The Elliott Wave Principle – A Critical Appraisal" Bolton refers to Garfield Draw, a student of R. N. Elliott, and author of *New Methods for Profit in the Stock Market*. In this publication no mention is made of Elliott's background by the notable Mr. Drew and a mere two pages of the 365-page volume are devoted to an explanation of the Wave Principle. It would appear that those who were unable to grasp the theories of Elliott merely dismissed them, while those who studied with him, kept his principles a well-guarded secret.

FIRST CONTACTS WITH WALL STREET

In 1966 we have the sudden appearance in print of Charles J. Collins. Having learned of Collins' previous association with R. N. Elliott, A. Hamilton Bond commissioned him to make a contribution to the 1966 annual supplement of the Bolton, Tremblay *Bank Credit Analyst*, such supplements being usually devoted to a dissertation on the current placement of the U.S. Stock Market within the Elliott Wave Cycle.

Collins tells of his first encounter with R. N. Elliott in late 1934. According to Collins, Elliott wrote to him from California in the autumn of 1934 claiming that a bull market in Wall Street had begun and the particular move was likely to carry the Dow-Jones Industrial Averages for a considerable distance. Elliott also proposed that Collins investigate his work on cycle theory upon which the forecast was based. Collins countered with the usual request, that Elliott go on record with his predictions for the period. Collins then let the matter rest.

At that time Charles J. Collins was the editor of a weekly investment bulletin in America distributed on a national basis. As is common to most publishers of investment advice Collins was subject to frequent letters and a stream of visitors all claiming to have developed "infallible" methods or systems for forecasting the stock market. I have had them in my offices over the past few years and have adopted an approach similar to that of Collins. In an effort to discourage repeated requests for assessment of these "beat the market" methods I usually suggest that the author of the system go on record with me over a complete up-and-down market cycle. If the record proved the method had some merit I would then determine whether or not to investigate the matter in further detail, possibly submitting the method to the London School of Economics who provide testing facilities. In practically all instances, at some point in the stock market cycle the system goes haywire and nothing further is heard from the author of the system. Collins makes it quite clear that Elliott and his work were one of three notable exceptions in his lifetime.

In March 1935 the Dow-Jones Rail Averages collapsed under the 1934 low while the Dow-Jones Industrial Averages shed over 11 per cent in tandem. According to classic Dow theory, a shuddering "sell signal" was produced and in Collins' mind it looked as if another so-called "infallible" stock market system was ready for annihilation. Obviously, with the disaster of 1929 still fresh in the minds of the U.S. investing public, the development scared the daylights out of most people. Completely unperturbed by the decline, Elliott cabled Collins on the very day the Dow-Jones Industrial Averages plumbed what subsequently proved to be an important low. As was always his way, Elliott dogmatically affirmed that the break in the market was over and that another leg of the bull market was just beginning.

As Collins was reading the telegram the Dow-Jones Industrial Averages were racing upward. However, the time stamp on the telegram clearly showed that Elliott had issued the wire two hours before the Dow-Jones Industrial Average had hit bottom. For the two months that followed, the U.S. market continued to forge ahead. So impressed was Collins with the accuracy of the Elliott forecast, not to mention his dogmatism, that Elliott was invited as the house guest of Mr. Collins at his splendid estate in New England.

Elliott accepted the invitation and the two men spent several weeks together thoroughly investigating Elliott's Wave Principle. As intriguing as the principle was the modest background from which it emanated. Elliott was an American citizen, but said he had been a wireless operator in Mexico before he was stricken with illness. Upon the instructions of his medical adviser Elliott was forced to move back to his original home in California, where, for almost three years, all he could do was sit on the front porch. For want of any other intellectual stimulation and in order to keep his mind occupied, Elliott began to study the stock market. He was a complete novice at the time. It was probably this factor more than any other which allowed him to pursue the subject with the necessary openness of mind. During his studies he covered the classical work produced by Dow, Schabacher and other analysts of the era. However, he discovered a pattern of previous share behaviour that went beyond the accepted methods of most analysts. Underlying the repetition of configurations which formed the cornerstone of most technically oriented methods at that time, Elliott discovered a form which seemed to account for the many times that the accepted patterns failed. In due course the wave theory thus evolved.

When Elliott approached Collins he was a fledgling in the securities industry, just trying his wings. He wanted to join Collins' organisation. However, it was the firm's policy never to base any decision-making on one single tool or on any single approach, while Elliott refused to allow any extraneous factors to deflect him from his Wave Principle. Collins offered to help Elliott set up on his own and was instrumental in obtaining some risk capital which Elliott was to supervise. Collins was then to edit Elliott's first monograph, "The Wave Principle" which was later supplemented by "Nature's Law", a more comprehensive document prepared by Elliott in which he added many philosophical points, including reference to Fibonacci Summation Series, all of which formed the basic rationale for the Wave Principle.

In these two monographs, Elliott postulates that all fluctuations in the stock market are fragments of a great rhythmic system of waves and cycles in ascending and descending orders of magnitude. This great rhythm is supposedly repeated in various forms of nature throughout the universe. Elliott himself was an agnostic, leaning towards mysticism, somewhat along the lines of thought established by the great W. D. Gann. It was Gann's contention that the stock market continually traced a pattern of perfect mathematical balance and that share price behaviour could be seen as being mathematically symmetrical when one finally established the starting point of the various forms of cyclical activity. Elliott also believed in this view and felt that the Fibonacci Summation Series formed the basis of all points of cyclical departure. I will describe exactly how the Fibonacci Series fitted into Elliott's scheme. It is remarkable how Josef Schillinger operating in a totally different area arrived at the same conclusion in his superb volume, *The Mathematical Basis of the Arts*. As we continue, the reader will no doubt be astonished at the manner in which this concept of mathematical symmetry weaves in and out of the various aspects of human behaviour.

ELLIOTT AND THE ECONOMISTS

Elliott explained the historic movement of share prices on the basis of irresistible cyclical forces acting over long periods of time. Obviously, he was not alone in his direction of thought, although he was the only man ever to apply these long-term cyclical influences to the stock market. N. D. Kondratieff, in his essay "Die langen Wellen der Konjunktur" discovered the 54-year cycle of economic life which confirmed the findings of the Dutchman J. van Gelderen, who in his book *Springvloed; Beschouwing Over Industriele Ontwikkeling en Prijsbeweging*, observed that in addition to the 10-year cycle discovered by W. Stanley Jevans in 1878, a much longer cycle of economic activity existed. Joseph Schumpeter later formalised the work of the main cyclical theorists: Kondratieff (54-year cycle), Juglar (18-year cycle), and Kitchin (4-year cycle). It was Schumpeter's concept in his *Theory of Economic Development* that each Kondratieff Cycle contained 3 complete Juglar cycles and 14 Kitchin cycles.

Professor Schumpeter wrote of his model:

> "No claims are made for our three-cycle scheme except that it is a useful descriptive or illustrative device. Using it, however, in that capacity, we in fact got 'ex visu' of 1929, a 'forecast' of a serious depression embodied in the formula: confidence of depression phrases of all three cycles."

Of the stock market Schumpeter states:

> "It is natural to expect that upward movement on the stock exchange will, in general and in the absence of unfavourable external factors, set in earlier and gather force more quickly than the corresponding upward movements in business, i.e. often come about already in the later stages of revival when things are beginning to look better every day, with new possibilities showing themselves. Similarly, it is to be expected that stock prices will turn before other indicators, i.e. when in the latter stages of prosperity limitations and difficulties emerge and it becomes clear that possible achievements have been fully discounted."

Whether or not Elliott was influenced by the work of the great cyclical economists it is not possible to say. From what one can gather, Elliott was intellectually honest yet there appears no mention of cyclical economic studies in any of his work. Should Elliott have drawn the conclusions in his work quite independently of those set out by Schumpeter and others, the nature of his findings becomes all the more intriguing.

THE GRAND SUPER CYCLE

Like Schumpeter's work relative to economic forces, Elliott began with one major long-term force which he sub-divided into lesser, shorter-term forces. However, his sub-divisions were far more detailed than Schumpeter's, the most distinct feature being the complete absence of any form of cyclical periodicity. He coined a system of terminology in order to classify the various wave dimensions. The major long-term cycle would be compatible with the Kondratieff Cycle. Elliott called this the Grand Super Cycle which spans a period of 50 years or more. The next cycle down the scale, obviously compatible with the Juglar cycle of economic activity, was Elliott's Super Cycle, spanning 15 to 20 years or more, depending on the duration of the Grand Super Cycle. Compatible with the work of Kitchin and his shorter term economic model, Elliott referred to the Primary Cycle, from which point there is a departure. Continuing his regressive categorisation we find the Cycle, Intermediate, Minor, Minute, Minuette and finally the smallest cycle of all, the Sub-Minuette.

Thus we start with a cycle of approximately 54 years in duration and continue sub-dividing downward until we arrive at the tiniest measurable degree. In London this "tiniest measurable degree" would be the hourly movements recorded by the Financial Times Industrial Ordinary Share Index. In Wall Street we have pure perfection, for the "Stock Master" provides minute-by-minute price changes in the Dow-Jones Industrial Averages, adjusted instantaneously for every single transaction that occurs in the thirty Dow-Jones Industrial Shares.

THE FIVE-WAVE CONCEPT

In addition to the concept of symmetry in descending magnitude with each of the larger waves divisible into smaller waves and still smaller waves still, *ad infinitum*, Elliott discovered that the individual components of the cycles of similar magnitude revealed specific behaviour patterns. While these behaviour patterns did not lend themselves to a fixed periodicity or repetitive patterns there was a distinct relationship to the various movements. Elliott concluded that, regardless of the magnitude of a cycle, a complete cycle consisted of eight distinct movements. Beginning with an upward cycle, Elliott discovered three basic ascending waves which he called "impulse" waves. Each of the first two "impulse" waves was followed by a wave which acted in correction of the entire upward cycle, and this correction wave itself consisted of two downward "impulse" waves interspersed by one upward corrective wave. In essence, we thus have an upward move consisting of five waves, three up and two down. Naturally the two down waves are of smaller magnitude than either of the preceding up waves. When we get to the fifth and final wave of the pattern we then have a major down move consisting of three waves; two downward waves interspersed by an upward wave, such upward wave being smaller in magnitude than the preceding down wave. This, in a nutshell, is Elliott's basic form. As we go on we will see certain behavioural characteristics of the various impulse waves and corrective waves, the relationships between which will establish targets, and help to serve in formulating an investment strategy.

The successful modern advocates of Elliott's work rank its precepts as comparable in importance to the work of Charles Dow, the granddaddy of all technical market theory. It has been said that Elliott's work begins where Dow left off. Charles Dow also discovered the vast cyclical forces which govern share price movements but was very limited in his classification. According to Dow, the basic force of the market was the primary bull trend which contained intermediate moves categorised as "secondary corrections" with the bull trend. The minor moves of the market were of little concern to Dow. Elliott's thesis of "three upward impulse moves" comprising each bull market would appear to be compatible with the three phase bull market concept developed by Dow. However, as has already been established, Elliott takes the work much further.

FIGURE 1

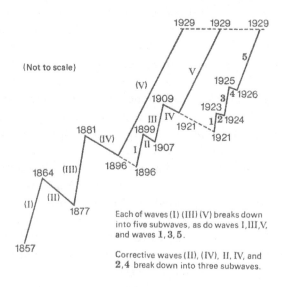

(Not to scale)

Each of waves (I) (III) (V) breaks down into five subwaves, as do waves I,III,V, and waves 1,3,5.

Corrective waves (II), (IV), II, IV, and 2,4 break down into three subwaves.

Some eminent technical analysts believe that the Elliott Wave Principle offers the only significant explanation of stock market history, accurately describing the upwards sweeps of share prices from 1857 to 1929, the corrective tidal wave from 1929 to 1949 then the great upsurge from 1949 to 1973 followed by the characteristic "Wave IV" plunge in Wall Street between 1973 and 1974.

In my view, the most astute of all technical analysts and probably the most pragmatic, is John W. Schultz, one of the few stock market technicians to develop a keen understanding of the Elliott Wave Principle. In his most excellent book, *The Intelligence Chartist*, Shcultz makes the following observations:

"The man who – so to speak – formally opened up Dow's trend structure was Ralph Nelson Elliott. He wrote very little about what he called the 'Wave Principle', and what he did write has long been out of print. He died in 1948. So far as I am aware, the only description of his theories currently available is one written by A. Hamilton Bolton."

"In formulating his wave principle, Elliott opened up not only Dow's trend structure, but a Pandora's box as well. He was willing to recognise four trend categories smaller than intermediate, and four larger than intermediate, nine in all including the intermediate category itself. And – to use our terminology – he instead that no trend category could have more than three components of the next-lower order running in its dominant direction. The idea must have been to set up a rigid standard of definition. But the fact is that trends develop more than three thrusts."

"Elliott got around this problem by permitting third legs to become very complex – that is, more thoroughly articulated than second and first legs. But, whether the rigidity of his theory yields a practical benefit or not is debatable. Attempts to implement Elliott's principle quickly run into mind-wrenching frustrations as multiple alternatives of definition suggest themselves."

Schultz's observations are quite correct. One of the most difficult aspects of The Elliott Wave Principle is magnitudinal classification of the waves and correct identification within the cycle. As mentioned previously the Elliott Wave Principle does not offer absolutes but alternatives. Anyone who seeks an absolute will find the Wave Principle quite unsatisfactory. But, equally, those who seek absolutes will ultimately find *all* stock market methods unsatisfactory simply because absolutes do not exist in the stock market.

THE NEED TO BE A GENIUS?

An approach to the Elliott Wave Principle is to accept this fact, and subsequently deal with the alternatives that are offered while building an investment strategy in accordance with the probabilities offered by the various alternatives. This sounds a lot more difficult than it actually is in practice. For example, if the "Wave Count" suggests we are beginning an upward move in Wave III or possibly an upward Wave V, the only factor to consider at that time is that we are beginning an upward Wave and that downside risks are limited. When confronted with these two particular alternatives the message that one would accept is the limitation of downside risk and act accordingly. At a terminal juncture the precise nature of the Wave is relatively unimportant. On the odd occasion one will find there are several alternatives offered by the Wave principle, where risk and reward are not satisfactorily definable. On those occasions, we merely step back and wait for the Elliott Wave pattern to produce a situation which can be defined with greater precision. I have always stressed the need for "masterly inactivity" on various occasions in the stock market. One need not seek a message with every single price movement every single day. Some price movements cannot be categorised until we move further on in the cycle. The most rewarding aspect of the Elliott Wave Principle is that when only one alternative is offered the probability for success is extraordinarily high as will be demonstrated as we proceed. The longer term investor need only deal with the longer term Wave developments whose terminal junctures are easily recognisable. There are two aspects of prime importance when embarking on a study of the Wave Principle. The first is mastery of the tenets which is not very difficult. The second is learning how to work with the Wave Principle, a subject badly neglected by practitioners. That particular subject is the primary function of this book.

At the 1972 *Investors Bulletin* Annual Seminar, James Dines said, "A genius by the name of R. N. Elliott developed something called the Elliott Wave Principle but it takes a genius to understand it."

Bear with me. You are about to become a "genius"!

Two:

Reality in the Stock Market

"It is, of course, easy from any set of statistics to prove that it is or is not. The National Bureau of Economic Research under Wesley Mitchell and Arthur Burns refuse to have any truck with thoughts about periodicity or form. Perhaps they are right. Perhaps all changes in the economic scene are due to accidental impulses which when totalled up come to a net of plus or minus factors without rhyme or reason. On the other hand, nothing in nature suggests that life is formless. If life has form, then it is a logical assumption that economics (which is a form of life) have form as well."

A. Hamilton Bolton

BEFORE EMBARKING ON a study of any of the technical tools of stock market behaviour one must accept some basic truths of the stock market itself. Failure to accept the truth of stock market action will result in a failure to comprehend the rationale for the methods being used, which in turn will result in a lack of confidence and, in all probability, an inconsistent approach to the method. There is nothing worse than a student of stock market behaviour who suddenly places all his faith in a particular tool, finds the tool lets him down on the odd occasion, then switches to another tool, and so on and so forth, until the results he achieves are totally random. The secret to stock market success is to find a tool with a high probability of success, stick with that tool and above all, be consistent in your approach.

$2,000 TO $1,000,000

During my lectures I often tell the story of my client in New York who parlayed a sum of 2,000 dollars, his life savings, into the sum of close to one million dollars. He had no extraordinary formula. He wasn't a dancer who pirouetted his way around the world with a "box system". All he did was place his total funds in the stock market whenever the yield on the Dow-Jones Industrial Averages rose to above 6 per cent. When the yield in the Dow-Jones Industrial Averages fell below 3 per cent he took all his money out of the stock market and put it in a savings account. He left his money in the savings account until the yield on the Dow-Jones Industrial Averages rose to above 6 per cent and then began the process all over again. Nothing could be simpler.

He had mastered three important principles: that of being inactive over long periods, that of consistency of approach, and the recognition of a high success-ratio criterion. Compound interest did the rest. He was a long term investor and it took him over 30 years to build his fortune. However, his method should provide an example. Even better results can be achieved with the Elliott Wave Principle if similar mental disciplines are applied.

My client was relying on the long term cyclical repetition of the yield factor. He wasn't particularly concerned with the time frame aspect, but merely the cyclical yield pattern. A theory based on cyclical repetition will always appear somewhat strange to those versed in the traditional approach to the socio-economic-world-of-finance type problems. The economy looks gloomy so we steer clear of the stock market. The economy looks bright so we are encouraged to participate in the stock market which will supposedly reflect the economic growth of the nation. A company turns in good results so we buy the shares of that company. All of this seems to be a perfectly logical approach but for some reason, share prices have a tendency to fall after a company turns in good profits. Furthermore, it is a fact that when the economies of various countries look their most promising, the stock market is usually on the brink of a disastrous decline.

THE FUTURE NOT THE PAST

There are reasons for this basic fact of stock market life. The stock market deals with the future not the past. Information that appears in today's newspapers is a report of events that have already occurred. According to the work of the academics who have studied behavioural patterns in the stock market relative to the dissemination of news, the stock market is totally efficient, and such is the speed of communication that there is no advantage whatever to be gained by acting on material which has been published for mass consumption.

Variations in share prices are the factors that lead to stock market profits, and the major turning points in the stock market are rarely confirmed by corporate earnings or the trend of business. If we examine a typical cycle, applying a basic Elliott Wave classification, we can see how this works.

As mentioned in the previous chapter, according to the wave principle, each bull cycle consists of three upward movements and two downward movements. Let's take a look at the London Stock Market over the past 12 months (see Figure 2).

FIGURE 2. F.T. 30. JAN 1975-FEB 1976

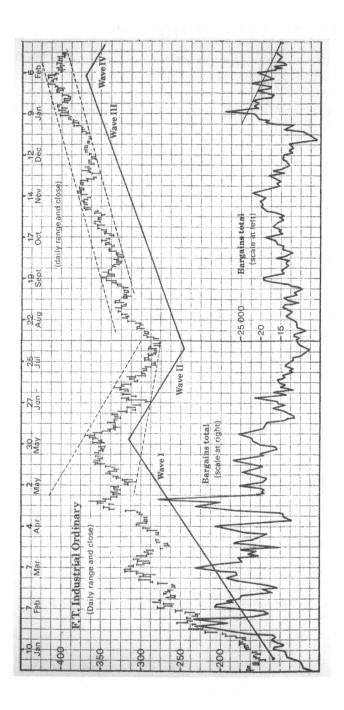

In January 1975, the U.K. economy was looking disastrous and the newspapers were printing a steady barrage of doom and gloom. But, as if by magic, following the announcement of the Burmah Oil crisis, in early January share prices started to rise. Not only did they rise but they virtually exploded. Very few members of the investment community believed in the rise and there certainly was a complete absence of any fundamental support for the rise. It was not until later in the cycle, after the stock market had almost doubled, that many began to find reasons for the move... after the fact of course. By June of 1975 the stock market had risen from the January low of F.T.30 146.5 to a peak of F.T.30 368. Since many felt there was little improvement in the economy over the entire period of the stock market ebullient advance, the only reason they could find for such a rise was that Britain was heading for hyper-inflation. Recollections of the manner in which the German Stock Market rose by 30 billion times its base level during the German hyper-inflation raced through the stock market. Just about the time this *a priori* judgement was receiving general acceptance, the market was beginning its first intermediate decline. Between January 1975 and June 1975, the British Stock Market completed the first Wave of what will subsequently be a five-Wave primary cycle. The second of the five waves began in June 1975 under the growing belief that the bear market was returning once again. By August 1975, the British investment community was forecasting a return to the lows of the previous bear market, and even lower. However, share prices began to rise again as the British Stock Market began "Wave 3" of its primary cycle, having complete Wave 2, the corrective down-wave according to Elliott.

1976 brought cheer to the investment community in Britain. The month of January produced a plethora of economic forecasts which pointed to a revival in the economy. Lead economic indicators were said to be turning up. Relations with the trade unions were improving. Share prices on Wall Street were doing well and all in all, a more bullish atmosphere couldn't be found. Fund managers were quickly reducing liquidity positions and the private investor began nibbling at shares once again. Finally, after 12 months of rising share prices, the investment community discovered the reason. There was about to be a brand new export-led growth in the British economy. In response to the general feeling, share prices rose throughout the month of January to reach a peak of 417 in the Financial Times Ordinary Share Index on the 30th. There didn't appear to be a cloud in the economic sky. Share prices then turned down and continued down through February and March. Wave 3 of the Elliott Primary was completed with the February-March move acting as Wave 4, the latter being given impetus by the resignation of Prime Minister Harold Wilson.

There were many bearish rumblings generated as a result of the political fiasco. However, the influence exerted on the stock market was short-lived with rallying action punctuating the end of March 1976. While there were many "bear scares" throughout the January 1975-March 1976 bull move in the F.T. 30, students of the Elliott Wave Principle would not have been deterred, for the end of the bull market was not likely to occur until a completion of the fifth and final wave.

CYCLICAL NATURE OF THE MARKET

The behaviour of the London Stock Market during the aforementioned period offers a test case example of the manner in which the inexorable cyclical forces act totally independently of the environment. History is replete with similar examples relative to stock market movements. News items can often cause extremities in the amplitude of a cycle, and sometimes affect the time frame of the Elliott Wave cycle, but never actually alter the cycle. More simply put, if the general psychological atmosphere is pessimistic, a bearish news announcement will cause an acceleration in any existing downtrend while a bullish pronouncement may mitigate the momentum of a down trend temporarily. If the general atmosphere is optimistic, a bearish announcement may slow down the momentum of the uptrend while a bullish announcement might accelerate the degree of rise. In both cases, the overriding major cyclical forces that govern the intermediate trend of the market will remain unaffected by daily fluctuations in share prices triggered by news announcements.

According to a study published by Draper Dobie, sources of price trends are foreseeable fundamental events, which account for 75 per cent of investors' motivation. The balance of 25 per cent is attributable to human response to those unforeseeable fundamental events which add "specific randomness" to share price motion.

Sources of share price trends which are attributable to the large bulk of investor motivation and thus affect the overriding cyclical forces can be summarised as follows:

1. Events of an historic nature which may motivate the buying or selling of shares.

2. Events which can be anticipated, influence the economy as a whole and have specific effects on industrial groupings.

3. Events which can be anticipated and which affect the performance of a particular company.

Short-term influences which cause "random noise" within the overriding trend, accounting for approximately 25 per cent of investor motivation, are those unforeseen events which fall in the following categories:

1. "Acts of God" – earthquakes, volcanic action, droughts, typhoons, fires, assassinations, insurrections, some government action.

2. Conflicting reports which attempt to forecast the unforecastable. With this category can be placed self-interest reports that are issued by government bodies and members of the securities industry relating to longer term economic forecasts.

3. Reports which are simply ill-conceived. In this category must be placed most stock market predictions that appear in newspapers, and predictions widely dispersed by individuals who use *a priori* judgement catering to herd instincts.

In this latter category, the rate of occurrence is frequent and the effect can be pronounced and sudden on the price amplitude but the effects are usually dispersed quite quickly and the time frame is not influenced to any major degree.

It should be permanently imbedded into the psyche of every investor that major and international events which attract massive response do

NOT dominate stock market activity on anything other than a short-term basis. To most investors, this is difficult to fathom. However, the study of cyclical movements in the stock market and the Elliott Wave theory over long periods should dispel the false belief that markets are actually dominated by these occurrences. Every day on picking up a newspaper one will find this or that national or international event being outlined as the cause of the day's stock market behaviour. Obviously, it is a total impossibility to trace the precise motivation of every investor. The alternative adopted by the press is to regard today's stock market action as reflecting the current news and local personalities instead of recognising that market action *leads* the business news events of the day and discounts *in advance* the business cycle.

The impact on market action of wars, global financial crises and all other similar events, does not alter the relationship of the cyclical time frame. Time synchronisation in coincident markets throughout the world continues; only the amplitude of the trend is distorted for temporary periods. The following diagram illustrates the economic cycle of Juglar and Kondratieff through the U.S. Civil Wars and the period following which included World War I and World War II. The chart is reproduced from the work *Cycles: The Science of Prediction*, by E. R. Dewey and E. F. Dakin.

FIG 3. WAR AND ITS DISLOCATIONS

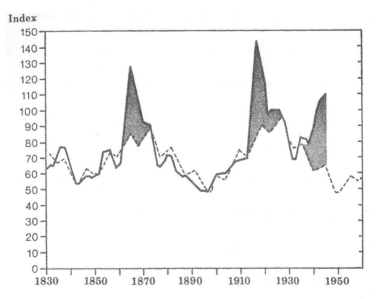

Fig. 3 shows distortion in the Wholesale Price Index in time of War. The solid line shows the three year moving average of the Index of Wholesale Prices in the U.S., 1830-1945. The broken line shows the synthesis of the regular 9-year and 54-year cycles. The shaded areas show the difference between the Index and the regular pattern for the periods of the Civil War, World War I, and World War II.

The 3-year moving average has been extrapolated to 1945. The shaded areas begin one year prior to the outbreak of the wars, since in a 3-year moving average the effect of the first year of war is extended one year backward.

It is interesting to note that in spite of the magnitude of the distortion, the timing *of the peaks happens to coincide with the normal timing of the 9-year cycle. It is also interesting to note how nearly equal are the distortions.*

The lesson to be learned from the illustration is the dominance of cyclicality in supply and demand markets, such as commodities, shares, etc., such cyclicality deriving from important basic rhythms in the world economy. Charles Dow stated that a bull market that takes place in one major country will usually take place in most countries having mature economies throughout the world. The concept of international economic cyclicality would explain this. With the growing influence of the multi-national corporations, the expansion of the Common Market, and modern communications of all kinds, the thesis set forth many decades ago appears even more credible.

Cyclicality in share price movements, as reflected by the popular share price indices such as the Dow-Jones Industrial Averages in the U.S. or the Financial Times Industrial Ordinary Share Index in London, is the summation (or combination) of all the basic rhythms in the individual economies and the common cyclicality of the components of these indices. Common cyclicality is the product of cyclicality in the individual issues, similar cyclical relationships in all issues, similar relative cycle magnitudes and their synchronisation in time. These factors produce trend dominance by the international stock market cycle or general sentiment, which in turn controls the majority of all share price behaviour. As mentioned, there will be deviations from the dominant trend due to the introduction of "random noise". As we develop the Elliott Wave Theory we will see how this "random noise" is compensated for.

TIME FRAME RELATIVE – NOT FIXED

While Elliott's work held certain common philosophies with those of the cyclical economists there was also a strict point of departure. Whereas Kitchin, Juglar and Kondratieff attempted to apply a fixed time frame to the behaviour of economic cycles, it was Elliott's belief that the time frame was only relative. Elliott was far more concerned with the behaviour of the component parts of the cycle, since the evidence he collected did not justify the repetition of share price movements over any fixed period, either short term, intermediate term or long term. We have no idea what methods Elliott used to collect and quantify his data. What we do know is that it took many years for the academicians with their elaborate computer programs to arrive at the same conclusion, to wit: share prices demonstrate randomness over all of the time periods which were tested. Obviously, the work of Elliott would corroborate the findings of Eugene Fama, Bachelier and Paul Cootner. While many "chartists" insist their work has never been suitably tested, the evidence provided by the aforementioned would appear to be overwhelmingly in favour of price randomness over fixed time periods. To my knowledge, only the work of Charles Dow and R. N. Elliott has been able to withstand the challenge offered by the academicians.

In a sense, the Wave Principle, developed by R. N. Elliott, is not truly a cycle theory. True cycles are observed repetitions of events at stated intervals. Aside from the economic cycles previously referred to, some examples of similar cyclical phenomena which have been discovered in the natural sciences are the 18-year sunspot cycle, the 9.2-year cycle of grasshopper abundance and the 17-year earthquake cycle. (There is an interesting 9-year cycle of electric potential gradients of earth-air current in London which could conceivably effect the amino-acid blood balances of individuals living in the city. A likely result would be a fixed periodicity rhythm of optimism and pessimism. I leave that subject for further investigation!)

Elliott had no intention of making any further contribution to the many cycles of fixed periodicity which were being discovered in his day. He believed that just because the stock market behaved in a certain manner, one, two, five, ten or twenty years ago there was no reason why it should behave in the same manner during a succeeding time frame of the same magnitude. He steadfastly refuted the "decentennial pattern" of Edgar Lawrence Smith who claimed to have discovered a 10-year pattern in share prices in 1938.

"It will work until it stops working," was Elliott's comment.

Not unlike the basis of Charles Dow's investigation, any classification of Elliott's work into the cyclical variety must be so quantified as having psychological derivations. The psychological theorists of market action are those analysts who place more stress on, or attribute more independent influence to, action and reaction, rather than cause and effect. Whatever the cause of a change in expectation in share prices, it is the consequence of that change, including the concomitant element of uncertainty, that the "psychological" theorist believes will trigger the next phase of the cycle.

Periodic repetition is irrelevant to the study of share price movements whose motivation is largely emotional. This was recognised both by

Charles Dow and R. N. Elliott. The tenets of Elliott state that the waves will unfold somewhat regardless of the time element, and that each subsequent wave will reflect investors' response to the extent and duration of the previous wave. Here is the only important time frame reference. That is, each wave must be related to the previous wave in terms of time, but need not follow a path of fixed periodic repetition. While this time frame reference may seem somewhat vague, it will prove to be the most important element in wave classification and offer the most pragmatic approach to the subject of cyclicality ever devised.

As the Elliott cycle unfolds one will find a series of "impulse moves" which ultimately rise to a level of excess due to over-speculation. These "impulse moves" will then give way to corrective moves so that the excesses can be eliminated and the cycle proceed. The time frame relationship is that a "corrective move" must lie within a similar time frame to that of the "impulse move". In other words, if we are dealing with an "impulse move" of two weeks in duration the "corrective move" should be of a similar duration, say seven or eight days. If we are dealing with an "impulse move" of two or three years in duration, such as suggested time frame cyclicality of bull markets in the U.S., the "corrective move" would take place over a period of 18 months or so. As we develop the wave theory, we will see the manner in which the time cycle is developed in accordance with the periodicity of the various moves in the cycle. What I have said thus far is primarily to demonstrate the difference between Elliott's concept and that of other cyclical concepts dealing with fixed cycle periodicity.

CLASSIFICATION OF WAVES

Probably the best way to gain a perspective of the time frame relationships is the classification of waves that appeared in the April 1974 issue of *Accountancy Magazine*, the Journal of the Institute of Chartered Accountants in England and Wales.

> "Elliott's actual classification of the various waves by degree in order of decreasing magnitude – designed to cover everything from the smallest imaginable wave formation involving the hourly moves in the index, for a formation lasting 200 years or more – were as follows:

- *Grand super cycle.* This was designed to cover the longest possible measurable time period. As of our current historical records, we have no concrete evidence of the completion of a grand super cycle, since Elliott's records only go back to the mid-1800s. According to Elliott, Wave I of a grand super cycle began in 1800 and ran to 1850, Wave II from 1850-1857, Wave III from 1857-1928, Wave IV from 1929-1949, and according to the principle, we remain in Wave V of a grand super cycle, which could stretch for several years more. Obviously, the risks are far greater for investors now than they were when we were at the early stages of the grand super cycle, such as the beginning of Wave III or even the beginning of Wave V.

- *Super cycle.* This is the next lower degree. Elliott claims that a super cycle of five waves began in 1857 (Wave III of a grand super cycle), following the depression of the 1850s. The five waves were completed in 1929. There then followed a corrective super cycle, running from 1929 until 1949. In 1949, a new super cycle began. We have completed four waves of the particular cycle with Wave V of a grand super cycle.

- *Cycle.* The wave pattern of the next lesser degree to the super cycle is that of the cycle. A breakdown of the 1857-1929 super cycle to cycle dimensions would give us the upmove from 1857-1864, the downmove of 1864-1877, the upmove from 1877-1881, the downmove from 1881-1896 and the upmove from 1896-1919.

- *Primary.* The period from 1896 to 1929 represents Cycle Wave 5 of the super cycle. If we break this cycle wave down to its primary wave components, we find an upthrust from 1896-1899, a downthrust from 1899-1907, an upthrust from 1907-1909, the downthrust from 1909-1921 and the big upthrust from 1921-1929.

- *Intermediate.* The intermediate waves of the long and glorious bull market that stretched for eight years from 1921-1929 can be subdivided into the upwave from 1921-1923, the downwave from 1923-1924, the upwave from 1924-1925, the downwave from 1925-1926 and the massive three-year upthrust that sent share prices soaring until they finally toppled over, from 1926-1929.

- *Minor.* By this time, readers may be somewhat suspicious of the historical data used as examples, doubting the application of the Wave Principle to the current environment. If we examine the upwave in the FT30 which began in February 1971 and ended in May 1972, we find the same five-wave pattern in repetition once again. Minor Wave I began in February 1971 and was terminated in May 1971. Downwave 2 began in May 1971, ending in mid-June 1971. Minor upwave 3 began in mid-June 1971, ending in September 1971. Minor downwave 4 began in September 1971 and was completed in November 1971. The longest wave, which is practically always Wave 5, began in November 1971 and was completed in May 1972.

- *Minute.* As can be seen, the minor waves will usually encompass the monthly movements of share prices, while the minute waves are likely to relate to the weekly movement in share prices. If we examine Minor Wave 5 of the move from November 1971 through May 1972, we find a Minute Wave 1 running upwards from mid-November to mid-January for a total of seven weeks. This is followed by a Minute Downwave 2 running down from mid-January to mid-February for four weeks. Minute Wave 3 starts in mid-February and runs until late February for two weeks. Minute Wave 4 runs downward from late February to early March for three weeks. Minute Wave 5 runs upward from early March until mid-May for eight weeks.

- *Minuette.* If we now take the period representing the last eight weeks of the February 1971-May 1972 bull move, this period representing Minute Wave 5 of Minor Wave 5 of Intermediate Wave V, of Primary Wave V of Cycle Wave III, etc, we can break the pattern down into its minuette components, which show the daily movements. Minuette Wave 1 began on 10 March at FT30 495.1 and ran for 12 days, reaching FT30 520 on 22 March. Minuette Wave 2 began on 22 March and ran for two days, bringing the FT30 down to 503.1. Wave 3

began on 27 March, running for 30 days, taking the FT30 up
to 540.3. Minuette Wave 4 then acted in a corrective fashion
for nine days, taking the FT30 back down to 419.6. The final
Minuette Wave 5 lasted 12 days until the top at 545.6 was
reached on 22 May 1972.

- *Sub-minuette.* The sub-minuette waves comprising the last 12
  trading sessions in the final stages of the bull move of May
  1972 reveal a Sub-Minuette Wave 1 lasting 12 hours, Sub-
  Minuette Wave II lasting five hours, Sub-Minuette Wave III
  eight hours, Sub-Minuette Wave IV six hours; the final burst
  of the Sub-Minuette Wave V was 19 hours long.

One can readily begin to see how Elliott's method completely
supersedes most other forms of pattern categorisation of share
price movements and, to say the least, clearly demonstrates the
obsolescence of the over-simplified bull market-bear market
fixation, which tries to establish a constantly recurring
periodicity of bull and bear market cycles into two and three-
year repetitions. The randomness of the time relationship in
classification amply demonstrates this point. For all practical
purposes, we have in the Wave Principle the ultimate work-a-
day series of stock market sequences."

Three:
Elliott... Pure and Simple

"The market was its law. Were there no law, there could be no center about which prices could revolve, and therefore, no market."

The Wave Principle (1938), **Ralph Nelson Elliott**

FROM ELLIOTT'S WRITINGS it would appear that he was well versed in the work that Charles Dow had developed while editor of the *Wall Street Journal*. By the time Elliott had formulated his work, the Dow Theory was some 50 years old and fairly well established in many quarters as having special forecasting significance. Elliott, no doubt, spotted the short-comings of Dow Theory, its imprecision and somewhat laggard characteristics. One of the primary problems of Dow Theory is that a trend is usually well established before one is advised to take action in accordance with the classic Dow Theory "Bull Signals".

It was Elliott's contention that since the store of information regarding stock market transactions has been greatly multiplied since Dow's original work, important and valuable new forecasting inferences could be drawn from certain behavioural characteristics of price movements.

A RHYTHMIC PATTERN OF WAVES

During years of compilation of statistics relating to share price behaviour, Elliott noted that the "wild, senseless and apparently uncontrollable changes in share prices from year to year, month to month, day to day, and even hour to hour, linked themselves into a law-abiding rhythmic pattern of waves". He claimed this pattern continually repeated itself over and over in sequence, ranging from the most minute hour to hour movements to massive market movements spanning many decades, as seen in the wave classification summary produced in the last chapter. By establishing the exact position of the current market's movement within the major cyclical force one could therefore determine whether the general trend of the market was in the incipient, mature, or mid-way development stage of any particular trend, planning one's investments accordingly. When discussing the Elliott Wave U.K. categorisation of the January 1975-March 1976 move, investors would have remained confident during the June-August decline of 1975 and the February-March decline of 1976, for only 3 impulse waves of that particular bull cycle had been completed. The mature stages of that particular movement would not occur until the fifth and final wave was reaching a terminal state. Thus investors could make their purchases with confidence during the aforementioned downswings which interrupted the cycle, and offered opportunities for the bargain hunters.

In many respects Elliott's principles are totally compatible with the workings of Dow Theory. Both men recognised that long and short term swings are part of the same movement. That is, Elliott noted, the small swings are an integral part of a swing of the next higher degree which in turn forms a part of a swing of the next higher degree still, etc. We thus start with hourly movements and build-up to the Grand Super Cycle. We can also start regressively, with the Grand Super Cycle working downward to the hourly movements.

It was Dow who established the analogy of the ocean tide, the waves forming a subordinate part of the tide, and the ripples in the water subordinate to the waves, each rising and falling with rhythmic regularity (a) from their own direct cause and forming cross-currents, and (b) being ultimately governed by the overwhelming tidal force. Perhaps one can more readily understand the several different trends of share prices which act concurrently with each other, sometimes counter to one another, by considering this analogy. In essence, the shorter term price movements which we have referred to as "random noise", basically caused by spontaneous occurrences, are the flotsam on the surface of the stock market ocean. Movements of this type, in two or three or more directions at once, and often opposing, are difficult to assimilate for many investors; but if we bear in mind the basic sub-division of three kinds of cycles, for the sake of simplicity – short, medium and long – and use the long to give us perspective from which to judge the short swings, and use the shorter swings to give us perspective from which to judge the longer swings, one can gain a greater proficiency in understanding stock market movements. Needless to say, comprehension or this simple phenomenon is mandatory if one is to understand the basis of the Wave Principle.

Elliott's work supersedes the work of Dow in the precise classification of the various movements in a completed cycle. One of the most fascinating aspects of the Wave Principle was Elliott's separation of larger corrective movements into the minor, minute, minuette and sub-minuette categories, all of which comprise a grand symmetry of share price movements which have been noted to be in effect since the 19th century in the U.S. and which can be observed dating back to the 17th century in the U.K. In these movements Elliott's basic pattern repeats itself over and over again, beginning with the sub-minuette cycles, upward to the minuette cycles, then upward to the minute cycles, upward still to the minor and then intermediate, and so on until we reach the Grand Super Cycle spanning more than 70-100 years.

ELLIOTT'S FIVE BASIC TENETS

The basic pattern which is the subject of this cumulative upward progression is quite simple to comprehend. Elliott's work can be summarised in five basic tenets:

1. For every action there is a reaction. Stock market movements in the direction of the main trend have been defined as "impulse moves". Stock market movements counter to the

main trend have been defined as "corrective moves". An "impulse move" is always followed by a "corrective move".

2. Generally, all "impulse moves" have five subordinate wave components while all "corrective moves" have three subordinate wave components.

3. When the main trend is upward, waves 1, 3 and 5 are deemed "impulse moves" and waves 2 and 4 are "corrective moves". When the main trend is downward, the first and third waves become "impulse moves" while the second wave becomes a "corrective move".

4. The action of the main trend can be taking place over a time frame of anything from a few hours to many years. When the main trend has completed a series of five waves the trend is reversed and a "counter move" consisting of three waves is expected.

5. Upon the termination of a move comprising five waves followed by a "counter move" consisting of three waves, we thus have the first complete cycle movement. This complete cycle movement will represent the first and second waves of a cycle in the time frame of the next higher degree.

BULL MARKET – BEAR MARKET

Well, that's Elliott's "pure"... now let's see if I can simplify it a bit. Elliott's basic configuration was the five-three pattern consisting of five waves in an overall upward direction and three waves encompassing a downward move. At this stage, for the sake of simplicity, we will act on the assumption that the five wave pattern is applicable to bull markets, bear markets having three waves. (No point in dealing with the variations and exceptions to the rule until we master the basic rule.) As I have demonstrated to members of my classes who have studied the Elliott Wave Principle, action based on this simple rule only will undoubtedly improve the performance of most investors. For example, there were several investors who were fortunate in having the foresight to purchase shares in the London Stock Market in January of 1975.

Many of these investors retired from the market too early in June of 1975 when only one wave of the bull market had been completed. Many more liquidated shares between February and March of 1976 when only the first, second and third waves of the bull market were completed. Students of the Wave Principle would still be holding their shares pending completion of the fifth wave. They will liquidate their holdings when this fifth wave is completed and not enter the market again until three complete waves of a bear market take place. The bear market that follows the 1975-7? bull market will be interspersed by an important rally, such rally being "corrective wave 2" of the three-wave bear market pattern to be expected following the bull market. Many investors will be tricked into re-entering the market when this rally takes place under the misapprehension that the bear market is over. Students of the Wave Principle will stand their ground recognising that the first rally in a bear market is often very deceptive, and realising that a third and final wave will be necessary to complete the next bear cycle when it comes.

In its purest form, the five-wave pattern is the bull market rhythm and the three-wave pattern is the bear market rhythm. The five-wave pattern entails three upward thrusts (waves 1, 3 and 5) and two recoils (waves 2 and 4). The three-wave pattern entails two downward thrusts and one corrective recoil in the opposite direction... a rally in a bear market.

The basic five-wave phenomena is best seen in Figure 4.

FIGURE 4

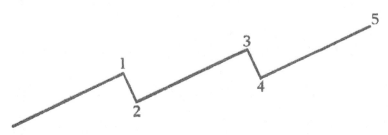

Rarely is the stock market as symmetrical as appears in the diagram, therefore treat the illustration as a guide only. We have a bull trend consisting of five waves, three in the direction of the main trend and two smaller waves which move counter to the main trend. As explained, the three waves in the direction of the main trend are "impulse waves" and the two smaller waves which run counter to the main trend are "corrective waves". Wave 1 is "corrected" by Wave 2. Wave 3 is "corrected" by Wave 4.

GROUND RULES

Now we can begin to establish a few characteristic rules which will help when using the Wave Principle as a forecasting tool. But first observe that the impulse waves are parallel to each other, and the corrective waves are parallel to each other also. These characteristics will later prove to be very valuable when applying the Wave Principle in the context of "channelling", the subject of a subsequent chapter.

Probably more important at this stage are the bottom levels of Wave 2 and Wave 4. It should be observed that in most stock market cycles Wave 2 will not retrace all of the ground gained by Wave 1 but only a proportion of it. When dealing with the subject of cycle amplitude we will be able to establish approximately what proportion.

Likewise Wave 4 will not retrace the total ground covered by Waves 1, 2 and 3, nor is it likely to retrace the ground covered by 3. In fact, we will find the depth of Wave 4 is usually related to the depth of Wave 2.

We can now establish the general rule: during an upward progression of five normal waves, Wave 2 of the formation will have an amplitude less than Wave 1 and Wave 2 will have an amplitude less than Wave 3, such is the nature of the corrective process. Furthermore, Wave 4 will usually terminate above the bottom of Wave 2.

For the sake of clarification, referring to the diagram, on the assumption that Wave 1 is say, 10 points in amplitude, when the downwave comes we act on the assumption that such a downwave will be less than 10 points. Likewise, if Wave 3 is 15 points we act on the assumption that Wave 4 will be less than 15 points. Generally, our Wave 4 will be closer to whatever the amplitude of Wave 2 happens to be. With these few simple concepts we are able to establish probable and maximum extents of the "corrective waves". It doesn't really take a genius to understand, does it? Let's continue by studying Figure 5.

FIGURE 5

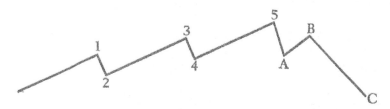

The five-wave pattern which has been illustrated in Figure 4 represents one complete upward phase of a cycle. To complete the cycle, what is expected to follow would be a correction of the entire move which began at the inception of Wave 1. A further rule we can establish is that when five waves are completed, the next corrective wave will be larger than any of the previous corrective waves, since the correction following a "Wave 5" acts to correct a cycle of greater magnitude. In Figure 4, Wave 2 corrects Wave 1 and Wave 4 corrects Wave 3. The correction that follows Wave 5 acts in correction of the sum total of Waves 1, 3 and 5 rather than just Wave 5.

In Figure 5 the corrective wave of the entire up move has been added, labelled ABC. As previously mentioned, the cyclical bear wave consists of three movements, two downward thrusts and one upward thrust. The upward thrust (Wave B) acts in correction of the first downward thrust (Wave A). The second downward thrust (Wave C) acts to complete the entire previously established five wave upward cycle. As the termination of Wave C, we then begin all over again with a new upward cycle, starting with Wave 1 and progressing through four subsequent waves of the next higher cycle. Before we introduce any further ground rules, I will demonstrate how to apply the principles outlined thus far.

APPLICATION TO INVESTMENT STRATEGY

Getting back to our previous example in Figure 4, we started with the suggestion that Wave 1 in that illustration encompassed say, a 20-point move in the D.J.30. When Wave 2 started, our assumption would be that it would comprise less than a 20-point down move. So should Wave 1 have begun at the D.J.30 level of 800, terminating at 820, we would "forecast" that the move downward from 820 would terminate above 800 on the principle that Wave 2 will not retrace the entire Wave 1 movement.

Also, for the purpose of illustrating the rule that Wave 4 would not retrace all of Wave 3 but related in amplitude to Wave 2, we suggested that Wave 3 be 30 points. Assuming a classic pattern, with Wave 2 consisting of a 6 point amplitude, we would then establish that the downwave that begins after Wave 3, when completed will be (a) less than 30 points, (b) more likely to be in the region of 8 points.

Now we can begin to fill in a few hypothetical numbers on our imaginary D.J.30 chart in Figure 4. Wave 1 begins at 800 and terminates at 820. We then have a 6-point down move which is Wave 2 taking us down to 814. Then comes the up move of 30 points to 844 for Wave 3 and this is followed by corrective Wave 4 of 8 points pulling us back to D.J.I.A. 836. Before demonstrating how we can make profitable use of the phenomenon we'll now add a further supposition, viz. that Wave 5 is of the same amplitude as Wave 1, lifting the index 20 points upward to 856. We're now ready for the "crash". What do we do as investors? How do we incorporate the overall scheme into an investment strategy?

In the first instance, under no circumstances would the investor have considered buying any shares on the move up from D.J.30 836 to 856 for this is a Wave 5 formation. He would have been quite happy to buy in the area of 814, realising his downside risk was no more than 12 points since Wave 2 would not retrace all of Wave 1. He would then be quite happy to buy following completion of Wave 2. He would also be quite happy to buy following completion of Wave 4 when the D.J.30 dipped to 836, realising that his downside risk was less than 30 points, and more likely 6 to 8 points, since Wave 4 would not retrace all of Wave 3 but would probably approximate the amplitude of Wave 2. In addition, the cycle was incomplete. Wave 5 was still to come.

The investor would naturally wish to begin disposing of some issues near the top of Wave 5 and would not consider making any repurchases until the D.J.30 had fallen a minimum of ten points. The rule which has been established is that the correction which follows the fifth wave, not only acts in correction of that fifth wave but also acts to correct the entire movement. Consequently, the downward wave following the fifth wave will be greater in amplitude than any of the preceding corrective waves. The largest corrective wave was Wave 3 involving a downward move of 8 points, thus the *minimum* expectation of the corrective wave following Wave 5 would be *more* than 4 points. We would then "forecast" that the *minimum expectation* for the next downward move in the D.J.30 would be 848 (856-8=848).

PROBABILITIES NOT ABSOLUTES

One should now note the strict departure from the ludicrous practice of most "chartists" who insist on predicting absolute levels in the D.J.30. I would state quite emphatically, that such predictions are utterly useless and totally beyond the realm of any reasonable probability. During our excursion with Elliott we will be using expressions such as the "maximum probable extent" of a particular move, or the "minimum expectation" of a move. When we say, the "minimum expectation" of the corrective wave is D.J.30 848, as above, we are in no way suggesting that the market will end up there. "Minimum expectation" means precisely that. The D.J.30 *may* end its correction at that point, but it could conceivably move downward much further. To those seeking the absolute, this may not be a satisfactory approach. I am confident those who seek such an absolute will never find a satisfactory approach nor will they ever achieve any degree of success in the stock market other than that which can be accomplished by selling pieces of paper with irrelevant predictions to investors.

The strategic aspect of dealing with factors which establish minimum and maximum probabilities, is that one never acts in a fashion counter to the risk factor. In the aforementioned example it would be totally imprudent even to consider a buying programme until such time as the market reaches its minimum objective. Likewise it would be imprudent to consider instigating a selling programme until the market had achieved a level close to its maximum objective; i.e. in the aforementioned case, the completion of Wave 5.

Many will now wonder why I have chosen to use such small hypothetical movements in the D.J.30 for my demonstration. I could have proposed that the hypothetical movement of Wave 1 in Figure 4 was say 70 points or so. I could have assigned movements of 110 points or so to Wave 3. The "corrective waves" 2 and 4 could have been proposed as downward moves of 30 and 40 points respectively. But the choice of sub-minute movements was quite intentional. I have attempted to present a situation which could be put into immediate practice, representing the smallest feasible amplitude which would be commensurate to what may develop as one watches the hourly action of the stock market.

PRACTICE RUNS

In subsequent chapters I will show how to use these hourly movements as a departure point in order to assist in wave classification. In the meantime, one can try a few practice runs with our Elliott Wave Principle. Attempt to determine the last important pivotal point in your favourite stock market index. From that pivotal point attempt to build a wave pattern, starting with the smallest movement. Naturally you will need an hourly chart of the index to do this.

Should the last important pivotal point have been, say, two weeks ago, you will want to build the hourly movements from that date. You will start with the sub-minuette moves that are the tiniest one can record. When you have completed the first cycle, you will find that you have also completed Waves 1 and 2 of the waves of the next higher degree, the minuette cycle. You then continue your monitoring of the hourly moves in search of a completion of a second complete cycle. When you have completed the second complete cycle based on the hourly move in the sub-minuette form you will also have completed Waves 3 and 4 of the moves of a minuette cycle, no doubt involving a longer time frame.

The final move that you will be looking for will be a "five-wave" in the sub-minuette cycle which when corrected will produce the first part of a larger wave which acts in correction of the minuette cycle. The corrective phase of the minuette cycle will be larger than any of the corrective waves within the upward phase of the sub-minuette cycle and will also be larger than any of the corrective waves which complete the three sub-minuette cycles.

Upon completion of the corrective wave of the minuette cycle, you will then have completed Waves 1 and 2 of the cycle of the next higher degree upward, the minute cycle. And so you will build, higher and higher, completing cyclical forces of greater and greater amplitude, while using the simple tenets established regarding the behaviour of the waves in order to plan your investment strategy.

I am fully aware that at this point in your introduction to the Wave Principle the tools at your disposal may appear limited, while the development of cycles of increasing magnitude may appear somewhat confusing. It is that particular characteristic of the Wave Principle that usually causes the most difficulty. In subsequent chapters we will discuss the aids that will help you in this respect.

Four:

"Like a Circle in a Spiral, a Wheel within a Wheel"

"By the Law of Periodical Repetition, everything that has happened once must happen again and again and again... and not capriciously, but at regular periods, and each thing in its own period, not another's, and each obeying its own law... the same nature which delights in periodical repetition in the skies is the nature which orders the affairs of the earth. Let us not underrate the value of the hint."

Mark Twain

RALPH NELSON ELLIOTT was neither a satirist who wrote books about boys under the pseudonym of Mark Twain nor was he a composer of the popular tune from which the title of this chapter was abstracted ("The Windmills of Your Mind" by Marilyn & Allan Bergman, Michel Legrand United Artists 1972). Elliott was a man of true genius, for the areas in which one will find reference to the Wave Principle in varying forms will stagger the imagination. It is doubtful if Elliott was influenced by Mark Twain or Mark Twain by Elliott, yet these two men from completely different walks of life arrived at the same independent conclusions, with Elliott developing a working hypothesis in the stock market from these conclusions. Unless one believes in reincarnation there can have been no mutual collaboration between Elliott and the Bergmans whose lyrics sing of the basic foundations of the Wave Principle. You may think these relationships are just coincidences, but as we delve more deeply into the subject, we will find firm corroboration based on much more than mere coincidence.

THE WAVE COUNT

In the previous chapter it was suggested to the reader that he use a day-to-day moving index in order to practise working with the "Wave Count", building hourly moves into daily moves, daily moves into weekly moves, sub-minuette cycles into minuette cycles, minuette cycles into minute cycles, minute cycles into minor cycles, and so on. In order to be sure the concept is fully grasped we will now work on the same principle, regressively, working downward, and on this occasion, introducing the time frame of reference.

Referring back to Figure 4 Chapter III, this time instead of dealing with small D.J.30 movements, let's assume that the diagram represents a complete Primary Cycle spanning many years. Remember, whether dealing with hourly, weekly, monthly, or yearly movements, the principles regarding the inter-action of "impulse waves" and "corrective waves" plus the "five up-three down" sequence, remain exactly the same.

So, for the purpose of illustration we will assume Wave 1 represents a move of say 240 D.J.30 points spanning a period of two years. Corrective Wave 2 represents a downwave of say 140 points spanning a period of 12 months. Impulse Wave 3 could represent a move of 400 points spanning 3 years while corrective Wave 4 might be a downwave of 180 points spanning 9 months. Finally, we have impulse Wave 5 which we assume represents a move of 220 points spanning 25 months. On the basis of this assumption the diagram would show a bull market lasting 8 years and 10 months involving a total upward move from beginning to end of 540 D.J.I.A. points.

If this were happening in reality, market analysts would insist that the first 24-month move was a complete bull market and that the 12-month move that followed was a complete bear market. They would insist that Wave 3 was a complete bull market and the 9-month move comprising Wave 4 was a proper bear market. Under the tenets of the Wave Principle, such classifications are out of place. Our main interest is wave relationship and categorisation. In this respect the time frame suggests a primary movement which will subsequently be divisible into an intermediate movement, then a minor movement, minute movement, minuette movement, and finally a sub-minuette movement.

Elliott's Principle is based on the conception that each of these primary waves together forming a complete movement can be sub-divided into waves of the next smaller degree. This can be seen in Figure 6.

FIGURE 6

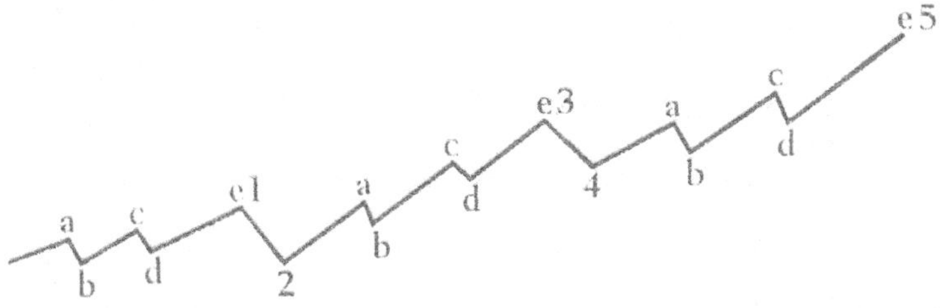

Note carefully that there are five smaller or intermediate waves labelled a, b, c, d, and e, whose sum total makes up the whole of Wave 1 of Figure 4 in the previous chapter. The same holds true of Primary Wave 3 and Primary Wave 5 each comprising intermediate a, b, c, d, e, waves whose sum total makes up the whole of the primary wave.

In the normal manner, Primary Wave 2 corrects Primary Wave 1, which consists of five waves of the intermediate degree. Likewise, Primary Wave 4 acts to correct Primary Wave 3 which also has five intermediate waves. (A breakdown of Primary Waves 2 and 4 has purposefully been omitted since the intermediate phases of Waves 2 and 4 require special treatment which will be dealt with subsequently.) Just as each primary wave may be sub-divided into intermediate waves, these intermediate waves can be in turn broken down into five sub-waves of the minor degree as illustrated in Figure 7. Note the manner in which Intermediate Waves a, c, and e, which resulted from a breakdown of Primary Waves 1, 3 and 5 in Figure 4, now have five tiny sub-waves of their own. We find that each primary wave has five intermediate waves and each intermediate wave has five minor waves.

If we had an unlimited amount of space we could break the pattern down further still, showing the five minor waves with five minute waves, the five minute waves having five minuette waves, and the five minuette waves having five sub-minuette waves. One aspect of the Wave Principle that will suddenly become vividly clear is that copious amounts of chart paper are required for a detailed study.

FIGURE 7

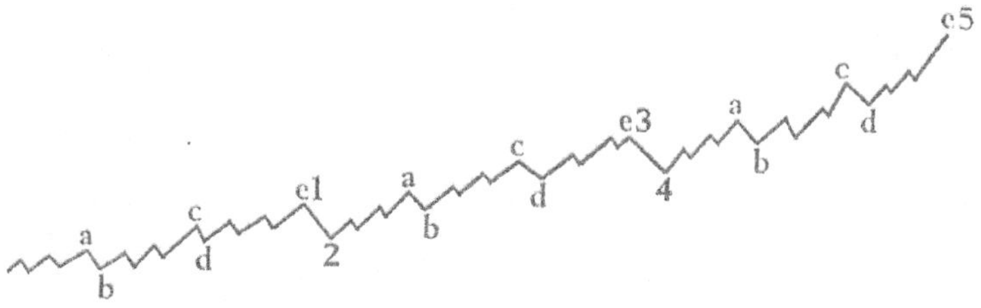

The primary waves would be equivalent to the very long-term bull and bear markets which span 5 to 10 years. In accordance with currently popular classification, this primary wave would probably encompass three bull markets and two bear markets. The intermediate waves would be likened to the generally popular classification of bull and bear markets that run from 2 to 3 years, and 6 months to 18 months respectively. The minor waves would be considered the monthly movements in share prices which run concurrently with both the intermediate and primary trends. The minute movements would be considered the weekly fluctuations, the minuette movements would be classified as the equivalent of daily fluctuations and the sub-minuette, hourly fluctuations.

BREAKDOWN OF PRIMARY MARKET CYCLE

Placing aside the time frame aspect for a moment, we submit a diagram of the breakdown of a typical Primary Market Cycle, sub-dividing downward to minute waves. The total number of minute waves in the complete Primary Cycle is 144. The total number of minor waves in the complete Primary Cycle is 34. The total number of intermediate waves in the complete Primary Cycle is 8. If we wished to break the Primary Cycle down even further we would find there are 610 minuette waves in a complete Primary Cycle and 2,584 sub-minuette waves. Needless to say, if we were to effect a breakdown from the Grand Super Cycle down to the sub-minuette the figures would become astronomical. For all practical purposes, a three-cycle breakdown for counting purposes is sufficient, i.e. a breakdown from the primary to the minute, the intermediate to the minuette or the minor to the sub-minuette.

FIGURE 8

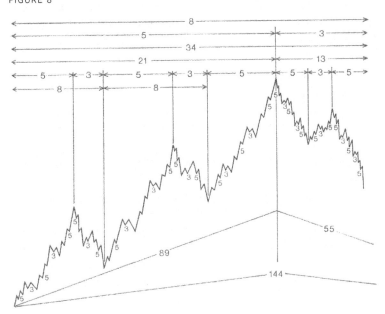

I have delved deeper than is strictly necessary into this wave breakdown in order to focus attention on the numerical relationships. In the illustration, one should note the numerical sequences of 3's, 5's, 8's, 21's, 34's, etc. What we see is the emergence of the Fibonacci Summation Series the function of which in the Wave Principle I will shortly introduce.

What sets the Wave Principle miles ahead of most other technical or "chartist" approaches is primarily the characteristic of design or form.

The waves take shape; they can theoretically be defined with precision; given any one degree of wave, once recognisable, it becomes possible to put these waves into the context of waves of the next larger degree, and the larger degrees thereafter.

For the reader who has followed the development of the Wave Principle thus far, startling implications should begin to appear. Given a reasonably definable five-wave pattern, it should be possible to subdivide each of the five waves into waves of a smaller degree. Conversely, given an hourly, daily or weekly series of small five-wave patterns, one should be able to forecast the continuation of the move until five waves of that particular time frame are completed. Then by using the first two waves of the time frame of the next higher degree, we can project the continuation of the subsequent five-wave pattern.

PIVOTAL POINTS

In the Wave Principle, we have a continually repeating cyclical phenomenon which allows one to judge the probable impact of the future amplitude and time frame of the subsequent stock market price movements as they develop, with some degree of precision and accuracy. If one can accurately assess the pivotal point of the initial primary wave (in London this can clearly be established at F.T.30 145.6, 6th January 1975) of a new cycle, subsequently determining the completion of the second corrective wave of the primary degree, one can then be fairly certain that the next series of impulse waves will make up the third and fifth primary, each of which will be running parallel to the first primary and comparable in time frame and amplitude.

The subsequent primary waves can be broken down into five intermediate waves and, if we commence our investment programme during the first intermediate wave of the third primary wave, there should be no danger of any major market reversal for a considerable period, in which case investment positions can be taken with relative security and equanimity.

On the other hand, when the fifth sub-minuette wave, of the fifth minuette wave, of the fifth minute wave, of the fifth minor wave, of the fifth intermediate wave, of the fifth primary wave, has spent its force, a formidable top is likely to have been constructed. When a move of such magnitude reaches its terminal stage, the destructive forces become aggressively dominant, producing a severe downward move long before the political or financial reasons for the change in outlook become apparent to the casual observer.

1984?

At this time I would like to interject a longer term forecast worthy of consideration in the context of the Wave Principle. In 1932 a new Super Cycle Wave was given birth in New York. Sometime during the 1980's the U.S. Stock Market will witness the final completion of the fifth sub-minuette wave, of the fifth minuette wave, of the fifth minute wave, of the fifth minor wave, of the fifth intermediate wave, of the fifth primary wave, of the fifth cycle wave of the fifth Super Cycle wave. Considering that the 1973-4 bear market was only a Cycle wave correction, the implications of the Super Cycle wave correction become obvious. But things could be worse. When we get to the year 2010 or thereabouts, we approach the period when a Grand Cycle correction will be coming up. For the time being, merely consider the projection as nothing more than an intellectual excursion on the Wave Principle.

I must emphasise that Elliott's Principle differs from other cycle theories in that it does not hinge upon the periodicity of recurring cycles. Within its framework, waves may expand and contract in time over very considerable periods. The "patterns" which have been referred to as cyclical phenomena are therefore far more flexible than those which one associates with more orthodox cyclical theories.

One of the most interesting aspects of all is that Elliott's Principle is based on *continued world growth*, even over the Grand Super Cycle period. The main direction of the Grand Super Cycle can be considered as always upward, the inner downward moves *always* being corrections of some degree. When we finally do have a correction of the Grand Super Cycle, the level to which the correction plumbs will still be higher than that of the corrective trough of the previous Grand Super Cycle. The same would hold true of the Super Cycle, Cycle, Primary, etc.

NORMALITY AND VARIATIONS

Elliott's basic concept is simple enough: the stock market expands and contracts in line with a set pattern akin to "shock" theory where the degree of response is related to the degree of subsequent action. The basic pattern is one of a five-wave forward movement comprising three upward waves and two downward waves. When such a five-wave pattern is completed, it is followed by a corrective pattern of three waves involving two downward movements and one upward movement, and so on, alternating until each degree formation of five waves becomes one wave of the next higher degree, and itself has a three-wave correction followed by subsequent waves of the same higher degree. This pattern is the basic of the Elliott Wave Principle in its simplest context, constituting "normal" market action.

Unfortunately, when everyone looks for the "normal" in the market, it just does not occur. What we wish the market to do is one thing; what it actually does is another. The foregoing illustrations, Figures 4, 5, 6, 7, and 8, are for demonstration purposes only and are not drawn to scale. If you have adopted the suggestion of attempting to plot the hourly movements of the stock market on graph paper, using the principles outlined, you may have found that the action of the market conforms precisely to the principles outlined. However, it is far more likely that you will find in the price movement taken from the market's actual behaviour that several interpretations may be applied, and the five wave movements you are seeking could be stretching outward to a greater number of waves, bringing you to the conclusion that the Wave Principle doesn't really work. When one goes beyond theory into practical application, significant distortions from the technical mode will always be found.

As we progress with our study of Elliott we will discover why these distortions take place and how they may be categorised. A further study of Elliott will reveal some extremely important variations to the basic tenets. These variations have been deemed to be more important than the basic hypothesis itself. For example, I have purposely left the breakdown of corrective waves for subsequent discussion. While corrective waves, with certain exceptions that will be noted, usually take place in three waves, the make-up of these corrective waves is subject to considerable variation. Likewise, we will learn that the fifth wave is often subject to an extension, and consequently the basic five-wave movements will often give the appearance of having a far greater number of waves than is proposed by Elliott's basic concept.

There is also another hitch of course – does one know at what exact spot one is in the wave formation? Is the down wave a "2" or a "4"? If it is a "4", is it correcting a sub-minuette cycle or a minuette cycle? Is impulse wave "1" actually an impulse wave or is it the corrective "B" wave of the previous cycle? At this point one may disagree with the attempted precision Elliott always insisted upon. In Elliott's opinion, all of the "i's" had to be dotted and all the "t's" had to be crossed without any room for argument or error. As will be seen, such precision does not really occur. The further we progress in time away from the important pivotal points in a cycle, the more will one's interpretation be subject to possible alternatives and variations *vis-à-vis* the wave numbers and the degree of cycle in which they are placed.

Just as the wave pattern unfolds as we go along, so will the complexities of the Wave Principle. This is probably why many students have given up in total despair and many other analysts refuse to take the trouble of giving Elliott more than just a cursory appraisal. In my opinion this apathetic stance is unjustified. There is an old stock market adage which says, "What everyone knows isn't worth knowing." When dealing with stock market techniques I would add a further adage, "The methods which are the easiest to comprehend, thus receiving mass usage, are generally not worth comprehending or using."

It does not require a genius to interpret the Elliott Wave Principle; at the same time one cannot just "look at it" in the same manner as "chartists" find a "double top" or "head and shoulders". It will require diligent study and a constant application of the various tenets which will be gradually introduced.

The remainder of this work will be devoted to (a) introducing the methods which are used to check, cross-check and verify cycle placement, (b) outlining the departures from the basic Elliott precept, and (c) providing practical application in forming optimal investment strategies according to the information provided by the Wave pattern.

At the risk of being repetitious I will be continually re-stating the basics of Elliott, as seen from varying approaches. I feel this is necessary in order that one can achieve a firm grasp of the nucleus of Elliott's work.

THE MARKET IS ALWAYS RIGHT

At no time have I made the suggestion that the Elliott Wave Principle is any simple means of going from rags to riches in no time flat in the stock market. I have tried to point out the difficulties in determining which of the wave degrees we may be in at any particular time; it should also be noted that events can sometimes occur which influence the amplitude and magnitude of the various different waves to the point that a clear perspective may be difficult to maintain.

What must always be quite clear to the student of the Elliott Wave Principle is that history is always right and the market is always right. If, from time to time, the analysis of the waves does not agree with history as it subsequently unfolds, then analysis, not history, is at fault. It is important not to be like the man who was killed in an accident maintaining his right of way, or the surgeon whose operation was a roaring success although the patient died.

IMPROVING INVESTMENT PERFORMANCE

While bearing in mind the difficulties you may encounter, it is still true that a mastery of the precepts we have covered up to now, albeit in limited respect of the complete Wave Principle, should help to improve your investment performance when using the Dow Jones Industrial Average, or any other index with mass sponsorship, as a timing guide.

If, during your current experiments, you find yourself lost in the tangled web of waves and sub-waves, merely stand away from the smaller patterns, awaiting the cycle of a higher degree to complete itself. As the days go by, you will find the wave pattern suddenly emerging with complete clarity. This may not occur in the hourly cycle you are studying. You might have to wait for a minuette cycle involving daily movements to develop. Then again, the situation may not clarify itself until one reaches the less sensitive movements in minute cycle or minor cycle. If you are a longer term investor you will probably have little interest in the sub-minuette and minuette cycles in any case. You will only want to keep a record of the developments of these cycles in order to quantify and clarify the position in the longer term cycle.

As an embryonic student of the Wave Principle, for the time being you will want to always be on the look-out for a completion of a five-wave pattern in degrees of minute, minor or intermediate time frames, adhering to the principle of "masterly inactivity" while you wait for the five-wave movements to be completed. Upon completion of these five-wave movements, then would be the time to consider selling action.

The amount you wish to sell will be directly related to the time frame of the cycle that completes a five-wave upward move. For example, unless you are a very short term "scalper", operating on a day to day basis in the market, you would probably have no interest whatever in thinking of effecting sales upon the completion of a five-wave sub-minuette pattern comprising hourly movements spanning three or four days. If you were a short term trader you would probably want to liquidate a few positions upon the completion of a five-wave minuette cycle spanning seven or eight trading sessions. As a short term trader you would always seek completion of a three-wave minuette correction before effecting purchases. This would be one of the few ways you could place the odds of short term trading in your favour. Unless you were able to buy at the incipient stage of the first wave of a minuette cycle, or during the third wave of a corrective phase of a minuette cycle, you would not make an otherwise attractive trade.

Intermediate term investors would probably ignore both the sub-minuette and minuette cycle, merely watching the movements in order to establish reference to the rest of the cycle. An intermediate term investor would wish to effect liquidations only upon the completion of minor and intermediate cycles spanning several months or years. The amount of liquidity to be raised would be governed by the particular cycle that was being corrected. Should a correction of a cycle spanning three or four months be taking place, it might be prudent to establish a liquidity level amounting to approximately 20 per cent of the portfolio. Should an intermediate cycle spanning one year or more be corrected, it might be prudent to raise the level to, say, 50 per cent. In the event of corrective action developing in a cycle comprising five waves each of one year or more in duration, the entire cycle spanning seven or eight years, the prudent course of action would be to remove all one's funds from the stock market and seek a low risk, capital protected medium of investment.

Long-term investors would only be interested in those cycles in Intermediate and Primary dimensions, effecting buying action during the final corrective phases, and remaining fully invested until the five-wave long term cycle completes its run.

We will now extend our studies towards anticipating the extent and duration of cycle waves, in order to determine the action likely to be required and the probability of success.

Five:
The Fibonacci
Summation Series

> *"So, naturalists observe, a flea,*
> *Hath smaller fleas that on him prey;*
> *And these have smaller fleas to bite 'em,*
> *And so proceed* ad infinitum. *"*

Dean Swift – 1733

B Y NOW YOU will have realized why John Schultz described the Wave Principle as hosting a variety of "mind-wrenching" exercises. So, let's take a breather. Relax a bit. Relax a lot. Let your mind wander. In fact, let your imagination soar. Think of the Universe, the Constellations, the Galaxy. Contemplate the beauty and form in all wonders of nature, the trees, the oceans, flowers, plant life, animals, even the micro-organisms in the air we breath.

Give further thought to the achievements of man through the field of the natural sciences, nuclear theory, penicillin, the brain scanner, radio, television. It may astonish you to know that all of these things have one item in common... the Fibonacci Summation Series, the mathematical rationale of the Wave Principle.

The history of the Fibonacci series dates back to the 12th century A.D., introduced by the famous Italian mathematician named

Leonardo da Pisa, or more likely, Leonardo Bigolla Fibonacci da Pisa. According to the record, Fibonacci toured the Middle East on a sabbatical, returning from Egypt with a mysterious set of numbers which later were to bear his name. Despite, or perhaps because of, the multitude of mysterious relationships within the series, it had never really attracted much more than curiosity from scholars. Recent theoretical developments in the field of non-linear mathematics place the series in a different light.

THE SERIES

The Summation Series itself is relatively simple, compatible with the entire Wave Principle concept. Starting with the number 1, the series develops as follows: 1, 2, 3, 5, 8, 13, 21, 34, 55, 89, 144, 233, 377, 610, 987, 1597, etc., stretching to infinity.

The series, entitled the Fibonacci Summation Series, can be seen to have several extremely useful properties and relationships:

1. The sum of any two numbers in sequence forms the next number in the sequence, viz. $3 + 5 = 8$; $5 + 8 = 13$; $1 + 2 = 3$; $3 + 2 = 5$; $89 + 144 = 233$; $987 + 610 = 1597$.

2. If we divide any number into the second number above it in sequence we will find the quotient of 2, with the number that is left over equal to the exact number resting immediately before the original divisor. For example, if we divide 21 by 8, the quotient is 2 with 5 left over; 5 is the number immediately before the divisor, 8. If we divide 55 by 21 we get 2 with 13 left over; 13 is the number immediately before the divisor, 21. If we divide 5 by 2 we get 2 with 1 left over. 1 is the number immediately before the divisor, 2.

3. The ratio of any number to its next highest number works out at 1 to 1.618. If we divide 987 by 610 the answer is 1.6180327. If we divide 144 by 89, the answer is 1.6179775.

4. The ratio of any number to the number below it works out at 0.618 to 1. If we divide 34 by 55 the answer is 0.6181818. If we divide 21 by 34, the answer is 0.6176470.

5. The ratio of each number to the second number below it is 2.618. If we divide 144 by 55 we get 2.6181818. If we square 1.618 we come up with 2.618 (2.617924). The reciprocal (1 divided by 1.618) equals 0.6180469.

6. We can classify the series as each number being related to the number before it by the formula:

$$1/2(\sqrt{5} + 1) \ (= 1.618)$$

7. The formula relating to each number to the number above it would be:

$$1/2(\sqrt{5} - 1) \ (= 0.618)$$

Academic to a study of the Elliott Wave Principle, but of certain interest to the mathematically inclined who wish to put this series to a further test, are the relationships discovered by the Russian mathematician, N. N. Voroslev. In his book, *Fibonacci Numbers*, Voroslev tells of further properties in this series which he discovered while engaged in research at the Leningrad Section of the Mathematical Institute of the Academy of Sciences.

1. The sum of the squares of any consecutive series of Fibonacci numbers from 1 will always equal the last of the series chosen, multiplied by the next higher number. For example:

$$1^2 + 1^2 + 2^2 + 3^2 = 3 \times 5$$

2. The square of a Fibonacci number less the square of the second number below it in the series is always a Fibonacci number. For example:

$$8^2 - 3^2 = 55$$
$$13^2 - 5^2 = 144$$

3. The square of any Fibonacci number is equal to the number in the series before it, multiplied by the number in the series after it, plus or minus the number 1. Example:

$$5^2 = (3 \times 8) + 1$$
$$8^2 = (5 \times 13) - 1$$
$$13^2 = (8 \times 21) + 1$$

One will also note how the plus and minus continually alternate. This phenomenon is an implicit part of the Wave Principle and Elliott's concept of alteration which states that complex corrective waves alternate with simple corrective waves, strong impulse waves alternate with weak impulse waves, etc.; this matter to be dealt with more fully in subsequent chapters.

W. D. GANN'S NUMERICAL APPROACH

Stock market students acquainted with the work of W. D. Gann will be aware of his attempts at applying mathematical balance to the stock market. In Gann's work we find time and amplitude of share price movements related to simple numerical sub-divisions. For example, one of Gann's principles deals with the high probability of a rally effort taking place when a share has fallen from its high to a point mid-way between the extreme high and extreme low of the share price over a protracted period.

When dealing with time studies, Gann attempted to anticipate changes in trend direction by relating the duration of a subsequent movement to the duration of the share price trend that preceded. Gann also used the sub-division of ascending and descending angles, sub-dividing them in terms of their probable importance as representing a possible pivotal point for a change in trend direction.

While these were the first attempts at applying a system of mathematical balance to share price behaviour, and, according to W. D. Gann's record of achievement with this method, the results were far superior to most other stock market trading plans, his work has always been difficult to quantify, while the simplistic mathematical principles employed leave many questions outstanding on the rationale of the work.

It is not known if Elliott was influenced by the somewhat obscure work of W. D. Gann. The only analyst Elliott ever referred to in his work was Charles Dow. Gann formulated his principles in the 1920's and 1930's. The Elliott Wave Principle didn't become known until the late 1930's. However, it would appear there is far more salient rationale in the use of the Fibonacci Summation Series as a common denominator of universal balance than there was in the simple sub-division of numbers employed by Gann. Whether or not this simple numerical series, known as the Fibonacci Summation Series, is actually the mathematical nucleus of universal motion as Elliott suggested, is naturally highly debatable, and in some quarters will prove intellectually unacceptable. However, the proofs that are offered seem to go beyond mere coincidence and would therefore be unworthy of total rejection.

The advantage of the Fibonacci Summation Series in its application to the behaviour of share prices lies in the fact that it deals in finite whole numbers, not in a concept of harmonic growth involving infinitesimal increments or differentials such as is common to calculus integration. In other words, it is a method of analysis which takes into account the characteristics of the available data.

THE FIBONACCI SERIES IN ART AND NATURE

In *Nature's Law* Elliott makes reference to the Great Pyramid of Gizeh. Many individuals interested in the occult insist the pyramid holds a divine message of revelation!

The pyramid's properties do offer some astonishing relationships to the Fibonacci Series. The height of the pyramid is exactly 5,813 metres, a number in the Fibonacci Series. The ratio of the base of the pyramid to its elevation is exactly 61.8 to 100.

Peter Tomkins, in his splendid book, *Secrets of the Great Pyramid*, takes the Fibonacci relationships visible in the structure of the pyramid even further. For all practical purposes the mathematics of the pyramid's structural relationships have resulted in the impossible function of squaring the circle. As students we were taught that the squaring of a circle offers an insoluble problem when we use the irrational value of π. However, the problem can be resolved if we use the Golden Ratio ϕ as a function. In the Great Pyramid of Gizeh one finds the function of the Golden Ratio in the relationships found in the triangle formed by the height, the half-base and the apthem.

It would appear that Fibonacci himself seems to have only used the series principally to explain a progression of numbers, such as the multiplication of rabbits from a single pair. Elliott notes a multitude of repetitions in nature. In Jay Hambidge's work *Practical Application of Dynamic Symmetry* to which Elliott refers, it is noted that the pattern made by the seeds at the centre of a sunflower has 89 curves. There are 55 winding in one direction of a logarithmic spiral and 34 in an opposing direction.

Other observers have noted the manner in which the series carries over into a myriad of man-made objects, living plants and animals. In a pine cone, the "grid" of opposing swirls which can be observed is composed of five lines in one direction and eight in another. In a pineapple husk one can find the ratio of opposing spirals to be 13 to 8. Examine a daisy head and you will no doubt discover the ratio of the swirling spiral of petals to be 21 to 34. One can also find similar relationships in the logarithmic or equiangular spirals in sea shells, tree growth, elephant tusks and the horns of the American Rocky Mountain goat.

The Fibonacci series transcends science and nature into art. Its relationships can be found in architecture through the "Golden Rectangle", in the shape of the Parthenon in Athens. As Joseph Schillinger observed, in his work *The Mathematical Basis of the Arts* referred to previously, the Summation Series appears in the painting of Leonardo Da Vinci, the music of Bach and the pulse of Keats's poetry.

Probably the most fascinating aspect of all is the manner in which the Summation Series can be used in the studies of "shock and instability", a concept which was instrumental in Niels Bohr's discovery of the process of cognition which guided him in developing atomic theory. Prior to Bohr's emergence as a scientist, he was a student of the philosopher Kierkegaard, his philosophic studies preceding his scientific work. Kierkegaard taught that "in life, only sudden decisions, leaps or jerks can lead to progress. Something decisive occurs always by a jerk, by a sudden turn which neither can be predicted from its antecedents nor is determined by them." No doubt Bohr was influenced a great deal by this philosophy.

EXAMPLES FROM *NATURE'S LAW*

The areas in which one can find examples of the Fibonaaci Summation Series and the 1.618 (Golden Ratio) relationships stagger the imagination. In *Nature's Law*, Elliott's magnum opus which he subtitled "The Secrets of the Universe" he cites further examples:

1. Our personal anatomy follows the Summation Series, in accordance with the five plus three pattern which characterises a complete stock market cycle. From the torso there are five extremities, the head, two arms and two legs. Each extremity can be broken down to the "cycle of the next smaller degree", of three sections. The legs and arms can be broken down into the next smaller degree also, the arms terminating in five fingers and the legs in five toes. These fingers can be further extrapolated into three sub-sections, the 5-3 pattern remaining throughout. (One may find an anomaly with regard to the big toe. However, in the case of monkeys, apes and other similar forms, the fingers and toes are the same in anatomical structure. The big toe of a monkey breaks down into three sub-sections as do the other minor extremities.)

2. In music we have the octave of 8 diatonic notes. We have the chromatic scale with 13 notes while the staff has five lines. There are three basic elements in music, melody, harmony and rhythm. Natural harmonies follow the Golden Ratio.

3. There are three primary colours. The blending of these three primaries produce all other colours.

4. The Washington Monument in Washington D.C. has a capstone with a base measuring 34 feet square with a height of 55 feet. The ratio is 0.618. The base of the shaft of the monument measures 55 feet square, while the rim of the shaft measures 34 feet. The foundation has 8 steps. There are 8 windows. The monument has three basic components. The base, the shaft and the capstone, the latter being the shape of a pyramid.

In *The Mathematical Basis of the Arts*, Schillinger contends that what we refer to as talent is in all actuality an innate sense of mathematical proportion peculiar to individual artists. This "mathematical proportion" can be seen in all great works of art, music, literature, etc. It is Elliott's claim that such proportion has its roots in the Fibonacci Summation Series which transcends all forms of human, animal and plant life, being the mathematical basis by which all activity is related.

FIBONACCI AND CYCLICAL BEHAVIOUR

Of greater interest to the student of share price movements – who should fully realize that such movements are the result of emotional rather than rational responses to day-to-day news events – is the manner in which the Fibonacci Summation Series can be found in the emotional cyclical behaviour patterns we experience.

For decades theorists have been attempting to correlate sunspot cycles and astronomical forces to share price movements and the stock market. It has only recently been discovered through the work of Dr R. Burr in his treatise *Blueprint for Survival* that sunspot activity has a direct effect on geophysical magnetic earth cycles which in turn affects the behaviour of various forms of life on this planet. The predictive value of this information is yet to be ascertained; however, it should be noted that sunspot cycles do conform to the Fibonacci Summation Series as do movements of planets and planetary relationships in our solar system. Furthermore, shifts in the earth's magnetic field force will alter the amino-acid balance in the blood stream which in turn can be related to shifts in emotional temperament which are likely to have an influence on mass behaviour patterns.

BRILLIANT... OR LUDICROUS?

Obviously, the sceptics, particularly the academicians who refute the idea of anything other than randomness in share prices, can find many objections at this point. Reference to "The Golden Ratio", "The Great Pyramids", etc., gives hints of numerology and mysticism, both of which are anathema to the pseudo-sophisticates of share price movements. The entire concept most certainly leans towards pseudo-science. Naturally, if one makes a point of searching for examples of the Fibonacci Summation Series they can be found in innumerable areas. In all probability there is a far greater number of phenomena in which the Fibonacci Summation Series *will not* appear. Many will question the logic of comparing stock market trends with the proportions of animal life and the structure of flowers, buildings, music and art. A surface appraisal will invite screams of "Where is the connection?" Such comparisons are likely to be deemed speculative and mystical. It is therefore no wonder that the academicians and pseudo-intellectuals will express contempt for this type of activity.

Unfortunately, however, those who do react in this manner run the risk of allowing their scepticism to swing too far. Not that mystical speculation is in the least deserving of a re-trial. Any method that lacks empirical evidence of rational justification certainly does not. However, a prejudiced intellectual suffers an extremely serious blind spot. The farmer in the fable of the boy who cried "Wolf" did not suffer from such a prejudice. He felt, in view of the boy's repeated false promise of the presence of a wolf, that empirically, it was highly improbable. At the same time he was not so self-opinionated as to deny the proposition further consideration.

The correct mental approach to the Fibonacci Summation Series and the work of Elliott as a whole is best summed up by William O'Connor in his brilliant work, *Stock, Wheat and Pharaohs*:

> "He apparently embodied ingenuity and brilliance, as well as the ridiculous and erroneous all at the same time. Should readers ever come upon any new revival and up-to-date revisions of Elliott's original works, it will be very advantageous to remember that this man eludes a unified classification as regards credibility. What he has given us is capable of revival and revision into foolishness, capable of revival and revision into brilliance, again both at the same time.
>
> It is customary to unify our attitude concerning the intellectual credibility of men. If a man doesn't know where Broadway is, there is a tendency to take that into account when he directs us to which way is uptown or downtown or the east side. But applying such an attitude to Elliott's Wave Principle, may cause us to discount the most brilliant aspect of him. His work will

not stand classification either wise or unwise, for it was both. But, on balance, the wisdom far outweighs its pardonable impurities."

OPEN MIND – SUCCESSFUL INVESTMENT

Studies in stock market psychology and the attitude of those investors who have been consistently successful in their speculative activities provide some revealing conclusions. Probably the most important intellectual quality for successful investment is the ability to keep an open mind, to recognise the finite nature of man's knowledge. The biggest mistakes are made by those who "do not know what they do not know". Students of modern capital market theory preach of the efficiency of stock market behaviour and the randomness of share price movements, assuming their computers are now capable of producing the final answer, not unlike the medical practitioners of years past who believed a headache could be cured by drilling a hole in the sufferer's head. The problem in both cases is the attempt to carry the technique of the period beyond its capabilities.

To accept the Fibonacci Summation Series as the final answer to share price relationships over time and amplitude would require faith as well as judgement based on empirical proofs. However, when one considers the empirical evidence produced to support various other aspects of stock market theory, one must come to the conclusion that we remain in a very "grey area" which remains to a great extent unquantifiable. So the only proofs that are of meaningful value are those related to achievement, and as will be demonstrated, the achievements of the Elliott Wave Principle as produced by its various practitioners go far beyond those which have ever been produced by any other method. This in itself should be sufficient justification for acknowledging the proposition that the Fibonacci Summation Series may offer clues, not only related to stock market behaviour, but to the behaviour of life patterns which heretofore have escaped recognition.

Six:

Applying the
Fibonacci Series

"All human activities have three distinctive features, Pattern, Time and Ratio, all of which observe the Fibonacci Series."

R. N. Elliott, *Nature's Law*

ACCORDING TO THE studies of L. Peter Cogan, economist and scientist, in his work, *The Rhythmic Cycles of Optimism and Pessimism*, the relatively high degree of timing, sequence, and amplitude tendency correlations between actual share prices, leading business indicators, private borrowings, and major business contractions, and ideal patterns of rhythmic repetition seem to confirm the existence of cyclical rhythms related to peaks in optimism and pessimism which govern mass behaviour patterns. The evidence available seems to refute the random walk theory of share price changes.

According to Cogan's thesis, monetary and fiscal policies do not appear to be the primary causes of the business cycle but merely act to modify the amplitude of the cycle and to some extent, the timing and periodicity. This view would certainly fortify the long-term cycle theories of Schumpeter and Kondratieff. In the case of the latter, the shorter term cycles, within the context of the long wave 54-year cycle, would vary in amplitude depending on the general level of confidence and liquidity, and on the timing, strength of action and ingenuity of political leaders, while the longer term cycle remains intact.

It would appear that 1929 and 1932 would have been major turning points in history regardless of who was president of the U.S., in the same manner as 1920 and 1974 provided periods of peak inflation regardless of the lessons that were supposedly learned during the intervening 54 years. Despite the accepted importance of military and political decisions upon the American economy, and the vast changes that have taken place during the last half century, with the economy becoming increasingly subject to Government intervention, the long wave economic cycle of Kondratieff, stated by Schumpeter to have applied to wheat prices ever since the 14th century, still persists. It seems more than a mere coincidence that this 54- to 56-year cycle, should be in such close proximity to 55, an integer in the Fibonacci Summation Series.

According to Elliott, *Nature's Law*, the mathematical basis of which is the Fibonacci Summation Series, has always functioned in every human activity, and waves of varying degrees occur whether or not machinery to record them is present. Obviously, Elliott was also something of an existentialist. When suitable data is compared with the cyclical patterns discovered by Elliott, the patterns of the waves become visible to the experienced eye.

Examples of data which can be subjected to Elliott Wave classifications are:

1. Extensive commercial activity represented by corporations whose ownership is widely distributed.

2. A general market place where buyer and seller may effect rapid transactions through representatives.

CHOICE OF STOCK EXCHANGE DATA

In *Nature's Law* Elliott clearly states, "In order to best illustrate and expound this phenomenon it is necessary to take, in the field of man's activities, some example which furnishes an abundance of reliable data, and for such purposes there is nothing better than the Stock Exchange."

The choice is obvious since in no other area has there been so much time and effort expended on predicting the future with such poor results. Elliott focuses on the examples of 1929. Despite the many forecasting methods then available, the bear market of 1929-31 still managed to wreck the investment community. Logically, 40 additional years of research should have done something to blunt the effect of the bear markets experienced worldwide during the 1970's. However, just as in 1929, hordes of investors were wiped out by the bottom of the decline and many investment companies, trusts, banks, etc., were annihilated. Forty years of stock market research produced very little reward indeed. The second reason given by Elliott for choosing the stock market as an area to illustrate the wave impulse common to socio-economic activity, is of course the great reward attendant on successful stock market forecasting.

"Even accidental success in some single forecast has yielded riches short of the fabulous," says Elliott. "From July 1932 to March 1937, for illustration, an average of thirty leading and representative shares advanced by 373 per cent. During the course of this five-year movement, however, there were individual shares whose per cent advance was much larger. Lastly, the broad advance cited above was not in a straight upward line but rather by a series of upward and downward steps, or zigzag movements of a number of months' duration. These lesser swings afforded even greater opportunity for profit."

If Elliott were alive today, he would have even more dramatic examples for illustration. Over the past five years we have seen the extraordinary boom in Australian mining shares which produced gains of up to 10,000 per cent in individual issues. We have watched the constituents of the F.T. Gold Mines Index advance by 900 per cent in less than three years, with some individual issues showing gains similar to those experienced by the aforementioned mining shares. And in the U.S. in less than 16 months, from December 6, 1974 to March 24, 1976 the D.J.I. Average went up almost 75% from 577.60 to 1009.21 with many individual stocks doubling and tripling in price. The first half of this decade will probably go down in history as offering one of the greatest fortune-making opportunities ever produced in speculative markets. But how many actually emerged with such a fortune? From the record, it would appear that very few actually took advantage of those extraordinary moves. The bulk of trading in gold shares didn't actually take place until the move was nearing its terminal stage. The same was true of the boom in Australian mining shares. Records which show the volume of transactions in both of these markets clearly verify the point. Although British equities staged one of the most startling advances ever, most of the British press expressed extreme distrust for the move throughout the upswing while the volume of trading was markedly low for the entire 13 months with the exception of a few bursts of enthusiasm during the early part of the swing.

The entire affair is summed up quite succinctly by Peter Bennett, fund manager and a director of Security Growth; "Never in the history of the London Stock Market has so much money been made by so few in so short a time."

A PSYCHOLOGICAL PHENOMENON

A factor which gives the Wave Principle additional credibility is Elliott's recognition of the true forces behind share price behaviour. The fact that most individuals do not succeed in their speculative endeavours, and the generally poor performance of the forecasting arm of the securities industry, is primarily because most individuals attempt to relate stock market behaviour to current events, whereas those events have little to do with future stock market performance. The stock market is constantly in process of discounting data before it actually occurs, so today's news has nothing whatever to do with today's share prices, even though journalists continually feature various news items in an attempt to make them conform to stock market action.

Elliott felt this aspect made his Wave Principle that much more important. He said:

> "Despite the attention given the stock market, success, both in the accuracy of prediction and the bounties attendant thereto, has necessarily been haphazard because those who have attempted to deal with the market's movements have failed to recognize the extent to which the market is a psychological phenomenon. They have not grasped the fact that there is

regularity underlying fluctuations of the market, or stated otherwise, that price movements in shares are subject to rhythms, or an ordered sequence. Thus market predictions, as those who have had any experience in the subject well know, have lacked certainty or value of any but an accidental kind.

But the market has its law, just as is true of other things throughout the universe. Were there no law, there could be no center about which prices could revolve and, therefore, no market. Instead, there would be a daily series of disorganised, confused price fluctuations without reason or order anywhere apparent. A close study of the market, however, as will be subsequently disclosed, proves that this is not the case. Rhythm, or regular, measured, and harmonious movement, is to be discerned. This law behind the market can be discovered only when the market is viewed in its proper light, and then is analysed from this approach. Simply put, the stock market is a creation of man and therefore reflects human idiosyncrasy."

The Wave Principle and its companion, the Fibonacci Summation Series represent the law or rhythm of man's response, which can be identified through share price fluctuations in the stock market and other areas where mass behaviour patterns manifest themselves through the forces of supply and demand. Once the waves have been interpreted the knowledge can be applied to any movement, as the same principle affects the price of shares, Government Securities, Grains, Metals, Cotton, Coffee, and other mass markets.

When the movements of these markets are studied with a view towards incorporating the Wave Principle three distinct features must be noted. Every series of actions and reactions will comprise Pattern, Time and Ratio, all of which will be found to observe the Fibonacci Series.

PATTERN

When dealing with the subject of "Pattern", the Fibonacci Summation Series will be applied to the actual "Wave Count". For example; normative behaviour of a complete stock market cycle consisting of a bull move and a bear move should involve the completion of 8 waves.

One will find the bull cycle consists of 5 waves, of which 3 are impulse waves and 2 are corrective waves, while the bear cycle will consist of 2 downward impulse waves and 1 corrective wave, all of which conform to the Summation Series. When we regress downward in the cycle, the cycle of the next lower degree should also have a breakdown of waves conforming to the Summation Series. In other words, the first impulse wave of the bull market should have five inner waves whereas the second wave, which is a corrective wave, should have three waves in the same manner as the longer term cycle which was our point of departure.

Should the impulse wave continue beyond the count of 5, normative behaviour has been superseded and we are then put on the alert that a further series of Elliott tools should be employed, such tools to be introduced in subsequent chapters. Basically, any impulse move should terminate with a wave count equal to one of the numbers in the Summation Series. An upward move that develops beyond five waves is likely to continue for three additional waves. A downward move which exceeds three waves is likely to develop two more waves; if these two waves are exceeded, a further three waves can be expected. If a count goes beyond 13 waves, counting both up waves and down waves of similar dimension, we can expect the move to continue in the direction of the main trend until 21 waves have been completed.

For predictive purposes, we can thus use a study of the wave pattern in order to tell us how much further a move is likely to develop before a counter trend gets under way. Generally, one should acknowledge that any move in a particular direction should continue until such time as a number in the Fibonacci Summation Series is complete. A major up trend comprising 4 intermediate waves, 2 up and 2 down, which in turn comprises 16 minor waves, would be an incompleted move, and the major up trend would have to develop at least five more waves before the up trend was complete and the next number in the Fibonacci Summation Series achieved.

A major Bear Market consisting of one intermediate down wave, comprising five minor waves, one intermediate up wave, comprising three minor waves, and part of an intermediate down wave comprising two minor waves would also be incomplete. Three additional minor waves will be necessary, bringing us to the number 13 in the Summation Series, in order to complete the move.

In order to verify the "Wave Count" one can begin with the waves of the highest degree observable, then descend downward to the intermediate, minor, sub-minor and even lower categories. Until the last wave in the lowest category reaches a number in the Fibonacci Summation Series, it is unlikely that the direction of the move in the wave category which formed the starting point will reach its terminal juncture.

Elliott states in *Nature's Law*:

> "From experience I have learned that 144 is the highest number of practical value. In a complete cycle of the stock market, the number of Minor Waves is 144, as shown in the following table:

Number of	Bull Market	Bear Market	Total	
Major Waves	5	3	8	complete cycles
Intermediate Waves	21	13	34	"
Minor Waves	89	55	144	"

> All are Fibonacci numbers and the entire series is employed. *The length of waves may vary but not the number.*"

The phenomenon and breakdown is best illustrated by the diagram in Chapter Four, Figure 8. It must be remembered that this chart is a model and one must never expect the stock market to behave in such a precise manner. As Elliott noted, deviations will occur in both time and amplitude, the individual waves not being likely to develop the regular patterns shown in the diagram. The illustration is intended to serve as a basic guide for the purpose of "counting" the waves. Suggestions that the market will behave with such rigorous conformity are not intended.

TIME

The next factor of the stock market behaviour where application of the Fibonacci Summation Series can assist in forecasting is time. In Chapter Three I briefly touched on the time span relationship and the manner in which it is used to verify the market's placement in the wave cycle. Fairly clearly, it would be unreasonable to classify a 2 or 3 week movement in the stock market as being a part of the same cycle dimension which spans several months even though the amplitude of such a short term move may appear compatible with a cycle wave of a higher degree. The "time" relationship would be the deciding factor in this case.

By using the Fibonacci Summation Series, superimposed on the time cycle, we can gain not only a clearer perspective with regard to cycle degree classification, but can also use the series to project terminal junctures and the degree of action likely to follow.

Investment Educators of Chicago, Illinois, were one of the few firms to develop the Elliott Wave Principle and present it in a form that could be taught to students. They referred to Elliott's "time" concept as representative of "isochronic time", joining points associated with a "constant time difference". While we do not have a "constant time difference" in the case of Elliott's work, we do have a constant time relationship in the form of the Summation Series.

When dealing with the time factor we must only make consistent comparisons. If we wish to project the terminal juncture of an intermediate move on the time scale we must use the terminal juncture of the preceding intermediate term move to make our projections. Likewise, if we wish to project the terminal juncture of a major move into time we must use the terminal juncture of the major move as a departure point. Similarly, a minor trend change can be projected in time when one uses the previous minor trend as a date for measurement.

When dealing with "time", price levels or the amplitude of waves is totally ignored. Time is only measured on a horizontal basis. There are only three important time periods to consider, and these are the durations of the major trend, the intermediate trend, and the minor trend. As you gain experience in looking at the various chart formations and dissecting the wave relationships, you will be able to recognise the various terminal junctures in their various degrees. By incorporating the Summation Series you will be able to perceive those points of measurement which will enable you to anticipate approximately when the various degrees of movement should terminate.

When attempting to determine approximately when a particular move will terminate we expect the time sequence, whether it be hours, days, weeks or months, to conform to the Summation Series. One should anticipate the possibility of very short term inter-day rallies or declines terminating within three hours on the assumption that such moves are counter to the overriding cycle. Any sub-minor move that runs beyond three hours will then offer a strong possibility of extending to five trading hours, the number five being the next number of the Summation Series. Should the particular move extend beyond five hours, a reversal would not be anticipated until such time as the move drew close to its eighth hour. Naturally, a move extending beyond eight hours would offer a strong possibility of continuing in the same direction for a further five hours, bringing us to the number 13 in the series. Obviously, an eleven-hour move would be incomplete. When incorporating this phenomenon in your short-term strategy you should immediately notice superior results by avoiding action during hourly movements which lie within a protracted periodicity of the sequence.

The same holds true for daily movements. No firm conclusion can be drawn during the first three days of a movement, regarding a sustainable trend. The series suggests a sub-minor trend is established, nothing more. A completed sub-minor movement can take place on any part of the first three days, the sequence of 1, 2 and 3 all being part of the Summation Series. However, when the movement goes beyond a third day we are then faced with a high probability that such a movement will enter its fifth day before completion. Carrying beyond the fifth day will present us with a further probability that such a move will extend for a further three days, therefore one should not consider action until such time as the eighth day of the move occurs. By now one can see how a move picks up additional staying power as it develops until the force is finally spent.

When dealing with longer time spans, the same method of approach should be adopted. A minor trend which develops into the fourth week of its movement will usually have at least one more week to go before reaching its terminal phase. Similarly, an intermediate term move of ten months duration is likely to continue in the same direction for a further three months. A major bull cycle of over 2 years in duration should continue for a further year. If such a Bull cycle exceeds the three year time span, another 2 years of the bull move is called for.

Several examples of longer time cycle moves have been provided by Elliott which confirm the validity of the application of the Fibonacci Summation Series to the time sequence.

The period from 1929 to 1942 (13 years) produced a Bear Market spanning 3 years (1929-32), a Major Bull Market spanning 5 years (1932-7), followed by an extended Bear Market spanning a further 5 years (1937-42). Elliott places special emphasis on this period from 1929-42. The entire pattern of development over that period comprises one massive "triangle". Each wave of the triangle is perfectly proportionate to its predecessor in accordance with the "golden ratio" of 61.8 per cent. All three factors, pattern, time and ratio are perfectly in accordance with the Fibonacci Summation Series.

At this stage several important qualifications must be made in view of the dogmatic insistence of "prediction" in favour of "probability" and "anticipation", by many who use chart patterns to predict price moves. When dealing with Elliott's time concept, the application of the Fibonacci Summation Series specifically, and the Elliott Wave Principle as a whole, the word which describes the approach is "anticipate". When a particular move stretches beyond the time sequence or wave sequence compatible with the Fibonacci Series, one does not "predict" the move will terminate at the next higher integer in the sequence, for quite simply, in accordance with the tenets of Elliott, it may not. One anticipates a terminal juncture at or near a sequence number and seeks evidence to support a terminal juncture when it appears to be taking place. It must be recognised that, should such a terminal juncture be absent, the move could stretch to the next higher integer in the series. The longer the move and the more advanced the wave count or the time count, the greater will be the probability of a terminal state. However, by no means should one attempt to force absolutes on this method of analysis. Fixed judgement and absolute predictions have no place in the Elliott Wave Principle approach to stock market behaviour.

For instance again, a minor movement of 30 years offers a strong probability of developing four more waves in the same direction of the movement. This does not mean the move will terminate when these waves have developed. One should anticipate the possibility of such a termination, bearing in mind the move could well extend to 55 waves, then 89 waves and even 144 waves. Similarly, a move which has gone in the same direction for 10 weeks offers a high probability of continuing in that direction for a further 3 weeks. This does not necessarily mean the move will terminate at 13 weeks. One should investigate the possibility of such a termination, subsequently comforted by the fact that if no such termination takes place during the 13th week, the move should run for a further 8 weeks, at which time one would then anticipate the possibility of a terminal juncture once again. Unless this aspect of imperfection is grasped, application of the Wave Principle will prove totally unsatisfactory.

Another aspect to consider is that the longer the projection in time span, the greater the chance of errors and multiple errors. It will prove far more satisfactory to make the projections as time moves along.

RATIO

We now come to the final aspect of the stock market behaviour to which the Fibonacci Summation Series is applied, viz. "ratio", or the proportionate relationship of one wave to another, both in time and in amplitude. In this instance we are only concerned with two mathematical factors, 1.618 and 61.8. This mathematical relationship is implicit in the "Wave Count" itself. As we know, a five wave movement is followed by a three wave movement running counter to it, three approximating to 61.8 per cent of five. An upward impulse wave comprising 144 minor waves will be followed by a counterwave comprising 89 minor components, 89 being 61.8 per cent of 144 in accordance with the series relationship.

When dealing with amplitudinal relationships rather than "Wave Count" relationships, Elliott cites several examples of application. For instance, the number of points registered by the Dow-Jones Industrial Averages between 1921 and 1926 (i.e. the first three waves of the Bull move) was precisely 61.8 per cent of the number of points during the last wave of the move between 1926-8. (It should be noted that according to the Elliott Wave "count" the orthodox top of the bull move began in 1928.) This relationship was repeated in the five waves up from 1932-7. The wave from the market top in 1930 (297 in the Dow-Jones Industrial Averages) to the market bottom in 1932 was 1.618 times the move from 40 to 195 which took place during 1932-7. The Bear market decline that took place from 1937-8 was 61.8 per cent of the 1932-7 advance.

In 1960, when A. Hamilton Bolton published the first definitive work on the Elliott Wave Principle, entitled, *The Elliott Wave Principle – A Critical Appraisal*, he stated,

> "Should the 1949 market to date adhere to this formula, then the advance from 1949 to 1956 (361 points in the DJIA) should be complete when 583 points (1.618 per cent of the 361 points) have been added to the 1957 low of 416, or a total of 999 DJIA."

In 1966 the Dow-Jones Industrial Averages advanced to marginally above the level of 999, but closed at 998.5, thus completing the long wave 1949-66 cycle, and unable to achieve this level again until many years later. Obviously, those who were *anticipating* a trend change in accordance with the principle of this proportionate projection would have profited handsomely.

CALCULATIONS AND EXAMPLES

When applying the "Golden Ratio" to stock market behaviour one assumes that since a Bull Market has five waves and a Bear Market three waves, the three-wave corrective move would be equivalent to approximately 61.8 per cent of the preceding Bull wave in time and/or amplitude. A Bull Market producing an index move of say 100 points over a time frame of say 2 years would thus be followed by a Bear Market involving a down move of approximately 62 points stretching over a period of about 15 months.

The simple formulae for calculating the proportionate ratio of time and amplitude relative to the various waves are as follows:

$$\frac{\text{Number of points in corrective phase}}{\text{Number of points in impulse phase}} = \text{Amplitudinal Ratio}$$

$$\frac{\text{Periodicity of corrective phase (hours, days, weeks, months or years)}}{\text{Periodicity of impulse phase (hours, days, weeks, months or years)}} = \text{Time Span Ratio}$$

As mentioned previously, it is vitally important to recognise the particular cycle time frame when attempting to forecast the termination of that particular cycle. Time span projections for a minor cycle will only apply to minor cycle time frames; the same holds true for intermediate and longer term cycles.

When using the formulae be sure that trends of similar dimension are accounted for.

For measuring the termination of a current upswing one uses the time frame of the last downwave in the same cycle dimension. For example, the Bear Market of 1972-5 in London lasted 138 weeks involving a decline of 399.4 F.T.30 points. Using the formula for proportionate relationship under the Fibonacci Summation Series ratio of 1.618, any succeeding Bull Market of normal distribution would involve an up swing lasting 223 weeks involving a total amplitude of 646 F.T.30 points from the January 1975 low.

In order to anticipate a likely terminal ending for a down swing in both time and amplitude we use the time and amplitude of the previous up swing as a guide. In the aforementioned example we used a major down trend in order to help establish a likely terminal ending for a subsequent major up trend. In this instance, we will use an intermediate up trend to help us establish the time and amplitude of the subsequent down trend.

On the 6th January 1975 the London Market began its major Bull move with the Financial Times Industrial Ordinary Share Index touching 145.5 inter-day, then reversing into one of the most dynamic surges of the century. The first intermediate up wave lasted 5 months, the peak of the intermediate wave being attained on the 6th June at F.T.30 369.6 inter-day. Normative behaviour for the subsequent correction of the intermediate upwave suggested a down move of 138.5 F.T.30 points (369.6 - 145.5 = 224.1 being the number of points in the up swing, and 224.1 x 61.8 = 138.5, being the number of points in a proportionate down swing) over a time span of approximately three months. In actuality, the subsequent decline lasted only two months involving a fall of only 92 F.T.30 points between the inter-day high on the 6th June and the inter-day low on the 8th August. Thus the decline was smaller than anticipated, involving sub-normal corrective action due to the generally strong undertone of the market.

THE "NON-ABSOLUTE" NATURE OF ELLIOTT

I have purposely chosen this particular example although many examples could have been selected from the 100 years of stock market history in Wall Street and the U.K. which fit the Fibonacci ratio to a more exact degree. Those seeking absolutes in their forecasting tools, i.e. precise "buy signals" and "sell signals", may find this aspect of Elliott unacceptable. According to the "norm" of many areas of technical analysis, the fact that the June-August decline failed to reach the projected targets would mean the theory is "wrong" or unacceptably inaccurate. Such is certainly not the case. When dealing with the Wave Principle one seeks to establish future normative behaviour patterns from which to establish broad guidelines. On many occasions these patterns of normative behaviour will be translated into precise market action. However, more often than not, these normative behaviour patterns will be either exceeded or fail to materialise due to a change in the character or the nature of price action. This in itself should provide further guidelines for students of the Wave Principle. The subject of "failures" (be warned... this is not what it sounds like) will clarify this point.

A corrective wave of sub-normal amplitude will generally indicate exceptional strength during the next impulse wave. An abnormal correction in amplitude will indicate the contrary. A sub-normal correction on the time span will act to sap strength from the succeeding impulse wave, making it shorter than usual. An abnormal correction on the time span will produce an extended period of consolidation providing a spring board for the succeeding impulse wave.

When there is a divergence between the amplitude ratio and the time-frame ratio of a corrective phase, the amplitude or extent of the price swing would take precedence for the purpose of future projections. In essence the shape of the "pattern" and the "Wave Count" should always be given the greater weight when attempting to establish future projections based on this particular aspect of the Wave Principle.

It should also be noted that the use of both the Fibonacci Summation Series and the ratios which are implicit in the series are intended to subordinate the basic Wave Principle, acting as a cross-check against projections based on aspects of Elliott's theory. The mathematical basis for the Wave Theory should not in itself be used to make "absolute" projections but rather to establish frames of reference which act as parameters for establishing subsequent behaviour.

STOCK MARKET HISTORY AND THE SUMMATION SERIES

Stock market history comprises endless repetitions of the series. The 1921 bottom in U.K. share prices was 21 years from the 1942 bottom. Similarly, the 1928 "orthodox top" was 21 years away from the 1949 bottom. The Bull Market from 1932 to 1937 lasted 5 years. The Bear Market from 1937 to 1942 also lasted 5 years. The 1921-9 Bull Market lasted 8 years. The first Wave of the 1937-42 Bear Market lasted 13 months. The Bear Market from 1929-31 lasted 3 years. It was precisely 89 months from the Bear Market bottom of 1921 to the "orthodox top" in 1928. More recent examples are the 13-month move from the Bear Market low of the 6th January 1975 to the peak of the third wave in February 1976. As mentioned previously, the first wave of that particular Bull Market was 5 months in duration, the combination of the succeeding two waves being 8 months in duration.

When dealing with the ratio, Elliott pointed out that the number of points gained during the first three waves between 1921-6 of the 1921-9 Bull Market were 61.8 per cent of the last wave 1926-8 preceding the "orthodox" top. In the five waves up from 1932-7 a similar pattern can be noted. The wave from the 1930 peak of 297 in the Dow-Jones Industrial Averages to the bottom of 40 in 1932, is 1.658 times the

1932-7 advance which took the DJIA from 40 to 195. Not only was the first wave of the 1937 Bear Market 13 months long but it spanned 61.8 per cent of the 1932-7 advance in DJIA points. In London we find the first three waves of the Bull Move from January 1975 to represent 68 per cent of the decline which took the F.T.30 down from 545 in May 1972 to 145.5, while the corrective phase is now nearing 61.8 per cent of the time span noted for the August 1975-February 1976 rise.

The series obviously occurs with astonishing frequency. However, it can be seen in the examples quoted that at times an important market bottom is found by measuring the time span between the two preceding tops, and at other times a top can be found by measuring the time span of the bottoms. On other occasions the periodicity of a down wave is found by measuring the time span of the previous up wave while the periodicity of an up wave is found by measuring the time span of the preceding down wave. The student of the Wave Principle should carry out all of these measurements in order to determine the various possibilities that can exist. The important factor to remember is that corrective waves should be approximately 61.8 per cent of the preceding impulse wave both in time and amplitude, while the succeeding impulse wave should be approximately 1.618 times the preceding corrective wave in both time and amplitude. When using the Summation Series itself, the corrective waves should be related to the preceding number in the Summation Series in time and amplitude. For example, if an impulse wave comprises 13 minor waves the corrective wave to follow should have 8 minor waves. Should a corrective wave last 5 months in duration, the succeeding impulse wave should encompass a time span of 8 months.

Seven:
The Trend Channel

"Charts not only tell what was, they tell what is; and a trend from 'was' to 'is', projected linearly into the 'will be', contains better percentages than clumsy guessing."

Robert A. Levy

A S WE PROCEED with our study of the Wave Principle we will steadily increase the number of tools at our disposal. Most of these tools will be subordinate to the basic Wave Principle, and will mainly be used to assist in establishing one's placement within the cycle, the primary objective being to establish the final wave of a Bull Market, and the final wave of a Bear Market so that appropriate action can be taken.

The manner in which the Fibonacci Summation Series can be used to anticipate the extent of a movement and the possible period after which such a movement will terminate, was demonstrated in Chapter Six. As stated, the use of this series is subordinate to the "Wave Count" and the price action, and is merely to be used in establishing possible terminal levels and dates.

Another tool to be used in a similar manner is the trend channel, discussed in Part III of Elliott's series of articles appearing in the Appendix to this book.

In the earlier chapters I outlined the manner in which the most simplistic aspect of the Wave Principle develops. During a Bull phase we find a series of five waves, each forward wave reaching a higher level than the previous forward wave, each corrective wave beginning from a higher level and ending at a higher level. The entire movement involves three increasingly higher peaks and two successively higher troughs.

In *The Wave Principle*, the first of Elliott's works published in 1938, Elliott states:

> "To properly observe a market movement, and hence to segregate the individual waves of such a movement, it is necessary that the movement, as it progresses, be channelled between parallel lines."

The operative phrase in the preceding statement is "and hence to segregate the individual waves of such a movement". Unlike traditional channelling methods wherein the chartist draws a trend line and assumes the Bull Market is intact as long as the trend line is intact, then assumes the Bull Market is over when the trend line is broken, in this instance the channelling technique is used to segregate the components of the Bull Market.

The usefulness of this method is best illustrated in the behaviour of the London Stock Market between January 1975 and February 1976, the first 13 months of the Bull move. Referring to the chart Figure 2 in Chapter Two, which depicts the movement of the F.T.30 during that period, observe the following:

1. Wave I of the move shows very little change in momentum, the tops and bottoms of the rise within fairly well defined limits throughout the upward thrust between January 1975 and June 1975, forming a sharp upward channel.

2. There was a distinct break of the trend channel during June 1975 thus establishing Wave II of the movement, which also remained in fairly well defined limits, producing a further channel.

3. In August 1975 the downward trend channel was broken and a new trend channel was formed, providing the easily definable limits of the cycle, and establishing Wave III of that phase of the Bull move which remained within parallel confines.

4. During February of 1976, the trend channel which established Wave III was broken, thus producing Wave IV and a further channel.

Clearly while there may be areas of doubt as to wave classification, if merely a "Wave Count" is employed, the incorporation of these trend channels goes a long way in helping to clarify the position.

LOGARITHMIC AND ARITHMETIC SCALES

It is useful to mention at this time that in larger formations, involving extended time periods, Elliott used almost exclusively logarithmic charts in order to make his calculations. For periods involving moves of 12 months or less, Elliott used arithmetic scales. Initially, Elliott called for arithmetic scales as the standard until he discovered as the longer term cycle unfolded, that the channelling technique began to lose its usefulness with the upper limits of the trend channel being broken.

As a general rule, when commencing with a study of short-term movements, one should plot the price action on arithmetic scales. As the price history moves along in time extending beyond 12 months it would then be wise to re-plot the price action on a logarithmic scale. In addition, if during the early stages of a move one finds difficulty in establishing the upper limits of a trend channel due to a market that may be highly volatile, showing a great deal of two way price action, it would be well worth the time spent to use two graphs, one with an arithmetic scale and one with a logarithmic scale.

The following examples reveal the totally conflicting results that can occur if the same data is plotted on arithmetic scales and logarithmic scales.

FIGURES 9, 10, 11, 12

If one were to plot a short-term move involving the price action as depicted in Figure 9 on a logarithmic scale, as in Figure 10 it would appear as if the trend channel was broken, whereas, in actuality, it would not have been. Similar would be the case for the longer term price action if one were to use arithmetic scales rather than logarithmic scales as can be seen in Figures 11 and 12.

FORECASTING USING TREND CHANNELS

In the article written for the *Financial World* on channelling (see Appendix) Elliott concentrates on the forecasting value of establishing a trend channel.

In commencing the construction of a trend channel one must first establish a suitable terminal juncture formed by the completion of a previous 3-wave corrective phase or 5-wave impulse phase. The terminal juncture should be checked and re-checked, in accordance with the rule for establishing time span periodicity, the "Wave Count", the previous wave amplitude, etc., generally incorporating all the tools introduced thus far and yet to be introduced.

Once the terminal point of the preceding move has been established one then waits for the development of two complete waves of similar degree in the current cycle. These two waves will provide three tangent points from which our trend channel will be initially formed.

The tangent points will represent the terminal ending of the previous wave, the terminal ending of the first wave of the new formation, and the terminal ending of the second wave of the new formation. Naturally, every available cross-check must be used in order to verify that actual terminal points in the cycle are being dealt with.

In the following diagram, Figure 13, we find two completed waves leaving three exposed contact points which are readily identifiable. The first exposed contact point would represent the terminal juncture of the preceding wave and the commencement of the first wave of the new cycle; the second exposed contact point is formed by the terminal juncture of the first wave in the new cycle, which also acts as the pivotal point for the beginning of the second wave. The third contact point is the terminal ending of the second wave which presumably will be the commencing point of the third wave.

For the purpose of illustration these contact points have been labelled "0", "1", "2".

FIGURE 13

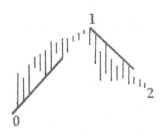

Always wait for the completion of these two waves before drawing your trend channel. A trend channel cannot be formed until the first two waves of a cycle are complete.

When preparing the channel, a tangent, which will be referred to as a "base line", should be drawn using the contact points of "0" and "2".

Once this "base line" has been drawn, a line parallel to it should be drawn, using "1" as the contact point, and extended some distance to the right as in Figure 14. This line will establish the upper limits of the trend channel.

FIGURE 14

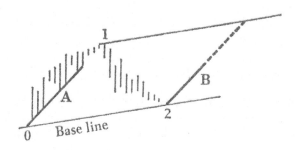

It will also be found useful if one draws a trend line tangential with the bottoms of the entire first wave movement, subsequently using contact "2" as a point from which one can draw a further parallel to the trend line between contacts "0" and "1" as seen in Figure 14. As I will demonstrate, whereas the upper trend channel line will help us establish probable targets relative to the amplitude of the succeeding waves, the channels within the channel will help us establish time frame references. These channels have been labelled "A" and "B".

When you have finished drawing the necessary lines, the completed trend triangle should appear as follows in Figure 15.

FIGURE 15

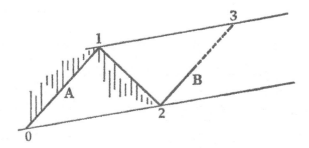

One will note a further line has been drawn between contact points "1" and "2". This line has been established by using the *peaks* of the down trend between "1" and "2" whereas the trend line between contact points "0" and "1" has been formed by drawing a line tangential to the *bottoms* of the up trend. Generally, when drawing trend lines we use the troughs as tangent points in an up trend, and the peaks as tangent points in a down trend.

We can now establish a probable target for the termination of the third wave in price and time, based on normal market behaviour patterns.

It is assumed the student is plotting line charts in the normal manner; with price on the vertical scale and time on the horizontal scale; logarithmic paper in the case of longer term price movements and arithmetic paper in the case of shorter term price movements. (The use of "point and figure" charts is not suitable for this type of analysis.) The likely terminal ending of the third wave can thus be found by extending line "B" to the top of the trend channel, and parallel with line "A". The vertical scale will give the price level at which the third wave will end, and the horizontal scale will give the approximate date of termination, i.e. at contact point "3" in Figure 15, and Figure 16.

FIGURE 16

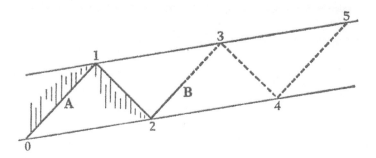

On the assumption that normative market behaviour continues and the third wave terminates at the top of the trend channel at the price and time co-ordinate established, one can then use the channel for plotting the possible terminations in price and time for the fourth and fifth waves. Using the end of the third wave as contact point "3" one draws a line parallel to that drawn between contact points "1" and "2". The point at which this line contacts the bottom of the trend channel will establish a probable price target and date of termination for the fourth wave, as shown in Figure 16.

In the same manner, once the fourth wave has been completed, and a contact point formed, a line is drawn parallel to the first and third waves. The point at which this line touches the top of the trend channel will provide the target for the fifth wave in both price and time, also shown in Figure 16.

FRAMES OF REFERENCE, NOT PREDICTIONS

The entire process of "channelling" would appear quite neat and tidy. Given the first two waves of any movement, the average "chartist" will now assume that the rest of the entire movement can be predicted. Much to his disappointment, he will soon discover such is not the case. While the process of channelling is indeed useful, it is certainly not intended that one should use it for making predictions and acting upon them.

Initially, one constructs the channel in order to establish *targets* in price and time, not unlike the manner in which economic forecasting bodies will establish targets for a particular phase of a growth cycle. One does not "predict" but rather establishes a frame of reference.

As the action of the market unfolds, we adjust our targets in order to compensate for deviations in the trend action. In essence, we establish a model which represents normative market behaviour, and then make adjustments to the model in order to comply with the action of the real world. Today, very few analysts have sufficient foresight to adopt such an approach, dogmatically clinging to preconceived judgements long after they are no longer applicable.

Whereas the dogma of most technical analysis insists that markets form a repetitive pattern and by awaiting repetitions of this pattern, one can "predict" the future, this is not the approach of the Wave Principle. Elliott recognised that share price behaviour can take on grotesque formations without any historic precedent... at any point in time the market can do anything it likes. Regardless of the behaviour of the share price movements, Elliott's theory states a basic form remains throughout, whether short term, medium term, long term or very long term. Recognising the basic form is the first step toward successful forecasting. Categorising and measuring the deviations from the basic form as the action unfolds is the second step.

DEVIATIONS FROM "NORMATIVE" BEHAVIOUR

Reference will now be made to Part III of the Appendix, Figures 8, 9 and 10. In employing the channelling technique, "normative" behaviour indicates that Wave 3 of a movement should terminate in the vicinity of the upper trend channel line that was drawn upon completion of the first two waves of the movement. Should Wave 3 terminate above the upper limits of the trend channel, the movement has taken on temporary strength and therefore modifications in the trend channel structure should be made. In the event Wave 3 terminates below the upper limits of the trend channel, a "failure" occurs and once again adjustments must be made. (The subject of "failures" will be discussed at greater length in a subsequent chapter.)

In the event of a significant deviation taking place in the price movement, with the termination of Wave 3 taking place at a level which is *2 per cent or more* above or below the trend channel line, the old channel is abandoned in favour of a new one to be drawn.

The new channel is formed by connecting the peaks of Wave 1 and Wave 3. A new base line is formed by using the bottom of Wave 2 as a contact point, then extending this line parallel to the newly formed upper trend channel line. In Part III of *The Wave Principle* which appears in the Appendix, Figure 8 shows both the old trend channel, shown dotted, and the newly formed trend channel. The original target for the bottom of Wave 4 is thus discarded and a new target at a higher level supersedes the original target. Naturally, the converse would be true should Wave 3 have terminated 2 per cent or more below the top of the trend channel. The adjusted trend channel would show less momentum and the target for Wave 4 would be lower down. Obviously, if Wave 3 terminates within a 2 per cent margin of the original trend channel, we will not discard the channel and the initial target for the bottom of Wave 4 would remain.

The object of every investor is to make purchases as early as possible at the beginning of every new major five-wave up-move, effecting sales upon the completion of such five-wave movement. Optimal results in the stock market are achieved in this manner. Establishing a target for Wave 5 is the most important aspect of Elliott's Wave Principle. As mentioned, the original targets that were formed following completion of Waves 1 and 2 gave us frames of reference from which to operate. The completion of Wave 3 may cause re-appraisal of these original terms of reference with the subsequent targets that are established by re-drawing the channel likely to reveal a greater probability of achievement than those anticipated during the earlier phase of the movement when the data was less complete.

When we have reached the terminal juncture of Wave 4 which could be either at the adjusted base line, above, or below it, the final adjustment in the trend channel is made, helping us to pin-point the all important peak of Wave 5.

The final, and most important channel, is thus drawn by using the bottoms of Waves 2 and 4 as contact points, adjusting and extending the base line forward. The peak of Wave 3 is used as the contact point for the commencement of the new upper limits of the trend channel. The line drawn from the peak of Wave 3, parallel to the base line drawn by connecting the bottoms of Waves 2 and 4 will thus provide the new upper limits of the trend channel, and the target in price and time for Wave 5.

Elliott's work on channelling as it appears in Figure 10, of Part III of the Appendix illustrates this point.

An important factor, neglected by Elliott, not only in the articles written for the *Financial World* but also in the 1938 version of *The Wave Principle* and *Nature's Law*, is the special treatment required for pin-pointing the peak of Wave 5, the time co-ordinate being the most important factor. The illustrations in Part III of the Appendix show parallel behaviour of all three impulse waves. This is very seldom the case and must not be treated as normative behaviour. Normative behaviour within a trend channel will show Wave 3 as being longer in both price and time than Wave 1. In this respect, it is most unlikely that Wave 3 will run parallel to Wave 1 although both upper and lower trend channel limits may remain perfectly in parallel.

F.T.30, JANUARY 1975-FEBRUARY 1976

Now referring to Figure 2, Chapter Two, the above-mentioned phenomenon can be seen most clearly in the behaviour of the Financial Times Industrial Ordinary Share Index during January 1975-February 1976. Wave I was extremely dynamic with the F.T.30 more than doubling between January 1975 and June 1975. Wave II was of normal proportions, involving a perfect "A", "B", "C" corrective wave presaging Wave III.

The character of Wave III was totally unlike Wave I. The angle of the rise was significantly smaller and the time period marginally greater. There would have to have been a sharp adjustment in the trend channel originally established by using the January 1975 bottom and the August 1975 bottom as contact points, with the June 1975 top as a commencement contact point from which to draw a parallel. In the "real world" of stock market action, Wave IV of that particular movement began in February 1976. When Wave IV is completed the new upper trend channel limits will be constructed by re-drawing a "base line" which connects the August 1975 bottom, the terminal juncture of Wave II, with the bottom of Wave IV, then using the February 1976 peak as a contact point, we would extend a line parallel to the "base line".

The question arises, when drawing a hypothetical Wave V, what references are used? We can either:

- Wait until the behaviour of the market shows an advance to the top of the channel, assuming further upward price action will continue until such time as we can reach the upper limits of the trend channel. In that case we would not be anticipating either at what level or at what period Wave V would be terminating. In fact, we would not be drawing a hypothetical Wave V at all.

- We can draw a hypothetical Wave V by drawing a line parallel with Wave III, using the bottom of Wave IV as a contact point. Where the hypothetical Wave V touches the upper limits of the trend channel we would check the price co-ordinate to determine approximately where the move will end, checking the time co-ordinate to determine approximately when the move will end.

- Instead of using the angle of incidence of Wave III for establishing a parallel reference for hypothetical Wave V, we can use Wave I. If we use Wave III for our parallel we would anticipate a rather long drawn-out ending to the Bull move. However, if we use Wave I as the suggested angle of incidence for which to draw the hypothetical Wave V, a very fast moving market would be anticipated with behavioural characteristics similar to Wave I.

The answer can be found in the normal characteristics of wave relationships. According to Elliott, the dimensions of Wave V should resemble those of Wave I in both price and time. Therefore, in constructing our hypothetical Wave V we connect the top and bottom of the trend channel by drawing a line parallel to Wave I which gives us the *minimum* probable extent of Wave V both on the price co-ordinate and the time co-ordinate. Figures 17 and 18 illustrate the point.

FIGURE 17

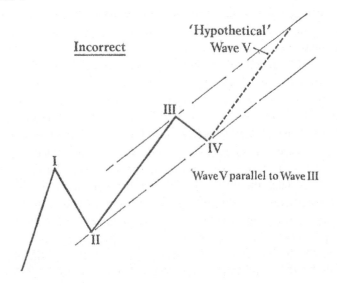

Incorrect

'Hypothetical'
Wave V

III

IV

I

Wave V parallel to Wave III

II

FIGURE 18

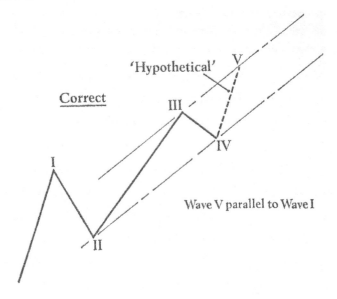

'Hypothetical'

Correct

III

V

IV

I

Wave V parallel to Wave I

II

To most students of technical analysis, Elliott's treatment of channelling will open up entirely new horizons for observations. Much of the value of Elliott's work lies in his close attention to detail and his examination of aspects of market behaviour which had previously gone unnoticed. One may be rather surprised at the way in which a simple concept such as channelling can be woven into what may be considered extravagant complexity, and to most, the discussion of channelling up to this point may suffice. Yet, Elliott observed further characteristics of market behaviour which extend the concept even further. These characteristics were observed with particular regard to the most important movement of the Bull Market, the final "fifth" wave. Normally, the fifth wave will terminate at the top of the trend channel, therefore, establishing targets at that level will on most occasions prove helpful. However, on several occasions the fifth wave will produce a "throw-over" above the top of the trend channel, referred to by Elliott as an "extension", such extension being subject to Elliott's theory of "double retracement". This subject, because of its frequency and importance, will be treated in detail in the succeeding chapter.

Eight:

Elliott, Inflation and the Fifth Wave

"When semi-log scale becomes necessary, inflation is present. If semi-log scale is used and inflation is not present, wave 5 will not reach the parallel line by a good margin."

R. N. Elliott, *Nature's Law*, 1946

ELLIOTT'S CONCEPT OF channelling was originally introduced in *The Wave Principle* published 1938, in which Elliott was quite insistent upon the use of arithmetic scales. It would appear by 1939, his insistence had waned somewhat and by 1946 when he published his magnum opus, *Nature's Law*, this view was completely revised. As mentioned previously, Elliott probably found the upper limits of his trend channels habitually violated.

In *Nature's Law* Elliott is quite emphatic on the use of arithmetic and logarithmic scales when applied to the channelling technique. "To employ one without the other, as a general practice, is erroneous and deprives the student of their value and utility", says Elliott. "The arithmetic scale should always be employed until log scale is demanded."

While Elliott still maintained arithmetic scales must be used for the shorter term movements, in the case of longer term movements the aspect of inflation was cited as a cause for extensions occurring during the fifth wave. According to Elliott, when the upper trend channel was violated by the fifth wave of a longer term movement, circumstances then "demanded" re-plotting on a log scale.

> "If Wave 5 exceeds the parallel line considerably, and the composition of wave 5 indicates that it has not completed its pattern, then the entire movement, from the beginning of wave I should be graphed on semi-log scale. The end of wave 5 may reach, but not exceed the parallel line.
>
> When semi-log scale becomes necessary, inflation is present. If semi-log scale is used inflation is not present, wave 5 will not reach the parallel line by a good margin."

R. N. Elliott, Nature's Law, 1946

(Note: Elliott uses the terms "log" and "semi-log" interchangeably.)

In our era, "permanent" inflation has been accepted as the norm. This is primarily due to the fact that inflationary trends represent the longest cyclical force in the economic time series, registering approximately 54 years from peak to peak. Anyone born during the post-1930 era will have experienced nothing but inflation, which grew slowly during the first 20 years of the cycle, the major inflationary acceleration taking place during the decade 1964-74. However, those individuals who may still be around and able to recollect conditions at the turn of the 20th century would have seen a moderate growth of inflation during the early 1900s, developing into an accelerated growth of inflation during the decade 1910-20 followed by 12 years of deflation from 1920 to 1932.

INFLATION IN BRITAIN

A peak inflation was recorded in Britain at 35 per cent in 1920, 54 years before the peak inflation of 1974 at 34 per cent. Between 1920-22 this inflationary rate had become "nil" whereas between 1974-76 the inflation rate was halved. Many will insist that the economic mechanism that we have today would preclude any such replay of the 1920 scenario. This is true, but only with regard to extent. The overriding cycle force remains unchanged. Whereas the period from 1920 to 1922 was characterised by a leap in the level of unemployed in Britain from 0.5 per cent to 16 per cent accompanied by a recession of horrific magnitude, no such event occurred during the recession following the peak inflation of 1974. The difference lies in the periodicity of the recession of the 1920s, where the measures to rid the economy of its inflationary excesses were compressed into an 18-month interval. Since 1974, the British Government has chosen to mitigate the effects of recession through intervention, by using monetary fiscal measures to blunt its effect. Thus instead of the "V" shaped economic recovery of the 1920s, during the 1970s Britain is experiencing a "U"-shaped recovery from the recession which follows peak inflations at approximately 54-year intervals. The effect is that unemployment is rising more slowly, the rate of inflation is falling more slowly, and the recession will be more prolonged. However, in the final analysis, despite the Government mechanisms that have been introduced over the past 50 years or so, the results remain the same with the longer-term cycle of inflation totally undeflected.

Recessions will act to correct the inflationary excesses which compound within the context of an economic recovery. Bull Markets reflect this compounding of inflation, while Bear Markets act in correction of speculative excesses in the same manner as recessions act to correct inflationary excesses, the stock market acting as a lead indicator in both cases. Obviously, the greater the inflationary excess the greater will be the subsequently corrective action in the economy, which in turn will be reflected in the stock market.

INFLATION IN THE U.S.A. AND FIBONACCI

The entire operation in process is demonstrated by the action of the Axe-Houghton-Burgess Index during the long super-cycle spanning 1857 to 1932. The Axe-Houghton-Burgess Index was the predecessor of the Dow-Jones Industrial Averages in the U.S. and represents the largest cycle degree for which records are available.

FIGURE 19. THE AXE-HOUGHTON-BURGESS INDEX 1857-1932

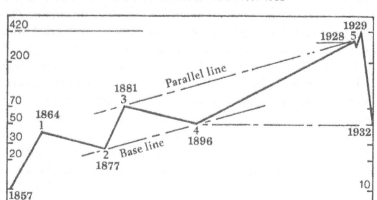

The chart has been drawn on the log scale since inflation was present during most of this period. The chart provided an ideal example of the manner in which the Wave Principle transcends exceptionally long periods of time, as does the trend channel which is a basic element of the Principle. The entire movement contains five waves with waves 2 and 4 resting on the lower limit of the trend channel, and Wave 5 falling at the upper limits of the trend channel, at which point an orthodox top began its development.

A factor which will subsequently prove of interest is the manner in which the 1929-32 Bear Market retraced all of Wave 5 which commenced in 1896.

In *Nature's Law* Elliott produces a break-down of this fifth wave which spans 1896-1928, divided into the five sub-waves of the movement.

FIGURE 20. THE AXE-HOUGHTON-BURGESS INDEX 1896-1932

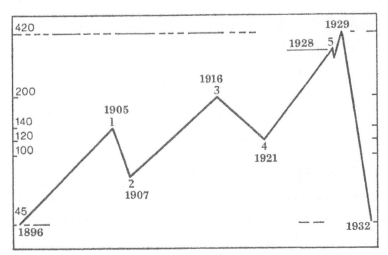

The behaviour of this long wave movement certainly lends credibility to the thesis of the Wave Principle. Note the manner in which the Bear Market of the movement from 1928 was halted at the precise bottom of Wave 4 – a normal correction demonstrating Elliott's theory of "double retracement" which will soon be discussed.

Elliott uses this long term phenomenon to demonstrate the application of the Fibonacci Series, citing the relationship of Waves 1 and 3 of the 1921-8 move as representing 62 per cent of Wave 5 in amplitude. During the 1857-1928 movement one can find a break-down of 7 Bull Markets and 6 Bear Markets, totalling the number 13 in the Fibonacci Summation Series. Most important however, is Elliott's view regarding inflation.

EARLY WARNINGS OF INFLATION

Elliott states that the presence of inflation during the 1920s was indicated by sub-normal Bear Markets during the period. He breaks down the 1921-8 Bull Market as involving three up waves and two down waves of a lesser degree, the down waves being of sub-normal amplitude. According to Elliott, warnings of inflation can be forecast by stock market behaviour in the following order:

1. Normal Wave 1

2. Sub-normal Wave 2

3. Normal Wave 3

4. Sub-normal Wave 4

5. Penetration of upper trend channel by Wave 5 on the arithmetic scale which often results in an "extended Wave 5".

EXTENSIONS

In Part VI and Part IX of the series of articles appearing in Appendix I, Elliott deals with the subject of "extensions", placing a great deal of emphasis on the fifth wave, a wave which is subject to Elliott's theory of "double retracement". Both of these principles will extend the range of tools which we are accumulating as we learn the complete Wave Principle.

There are certain rules regarding extensions which will help practitioners of the Elliott Wave Principle if they are adhered to. At all times, the important problem is in attempting to pinpoint the terminal phase of Wave 5 in any cycle degree, for the corrective action which follows Wave 5 will be greater than any experienced during the preceding run of the cycle.

Normative behaviour of Wave 5 has already been established. Over the shorter term (less than 12 months) Wave 5 should remain within the confines of a trend channel drawn on an arithmetic scale. Over the longer term, the confines would be established by the upper trend line on a logarithmic scale. Wave 5 should be shorter than Wave 3 and approximate the dimensions of Wave 1 in time and amplitude.

The first indications that we receive with regard to an extension developing in Wave 5 occur if the amplitude and/or time span of Waves 2 and 4 are sub-normal. A factor which would preclude the possibility of an extended Wave 5 would be an "extension" occurring in either of the preceding impulse Waves 1 or 3. While extensions usually occur in Wave 5 they can occur in either Wave 1 or 3. They hardly ever occur in more than one impulse wave of a movement.

Extensions can only occur in new territory of the current cycle. Corrective Waves 2 and 4 are therefore never subject to extensions.

Naturally, one must be quite sure whether one is in a major downward cycle or major upward cycle, and this is ascertained by the nature of the impulse move. If the pattern structure reveals five downward waves and three upward waves, the cycle is clearly downward. Impulse Waves 1, 3 and 5 of the downward cycle could then be subject to extensions. The "A", "B", "C" upward corrective waves in a downward cycle would not be subject to extensions.

Figure 21 serves to show the nature of the behaviour patterns when extensions occur in the various impulse waves.

FIGURE 21

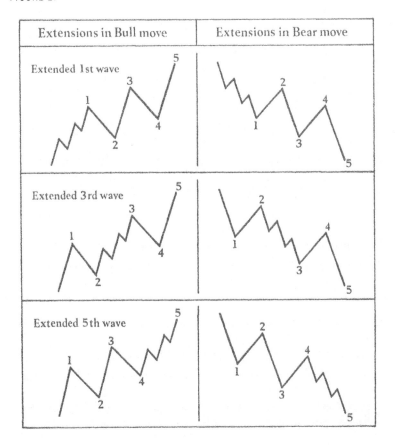

On rare occasions, an extension will occur comprising waves, all of approximately equal size, as in the following example (Figure 22).

FIGURE 22

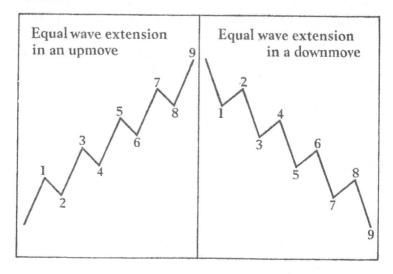

It is vitally important to recognise extensions when they occur since serious mistakes in counting the wave formation will result if these extended waves go unnoticed. When an extended wave occurs, the move takes on a count of "nine" rather than the usual five. In the case of an extended first wave, one finds five waves in the first wave with four waves of the same degree that follow. In the case of an extended third wave, the first two waves comprise the normal count. Wave 3 has a five-wave count to which waves 4 and 5 are added. When an extension occurs in the fifth wave it is somewhat less troublesome. The five waves of the extension are simply added to the four waves preceding.

Only on the odd occasion has Elliott made reference to volume characteristics in helping to identify wave movements. In the case of an extension one can gain corroboratory evidence from the volume figures. Volume tends to expand during an extension. In *The Wave Principle* Elliott states:

"Volume tends to climb on a throw-over, and when this throw-
over is by the fifth Intermediate Wave of a Primary movement,
volume should be very heavy."

In the Bull Market that began in January 1975 in London, such was
the strength of the initial up swing that an extension in the first wave
developed, with volume soaring to record levels when the extension
got underway. At the time of writing, June 1976, volume of trading
has yet to reach the levels recorded at the earlier part of the Bull
Market.

Generally, an extension can be seen as either a five-wave pattern with
an elongated wave, or a nine-wave pattern with approximately equal
components, the latter formation being somewhat difficult to detect,
but also quite rare. The wave which is most likely to be subject to an
extension is the fifth wave.

Verification of a first wave extension is relatively simple, once the third
wave of the same cycle degree has been completed. The first sign that
an extension may be taking place in a first wave would be the
penetration of the trend channel on arithmetic scales. It is most likely
that one would be using arithmetic scales at the beginning of a
movement. As the subsequent action of the market unfolds, should
Wave 3 fall appreciably short of the dimension of the first wave, it is
likely that an extended wave has developed in the first impulse move,
precluding an extension of the fifth wave. One should then check the
wave count very carefully. While such a reassessment of the
components of the first wave may not appear to be of much forecasting
value, it should be remembered that if a first wave becomes subject to
an extension the subsequent impulse moves are very likely to be
unextended. One can then act with greater confidence when a five-
wave movement draws closer to the upper limits of a trend channel, if
either the first wave or the third wave has been extended, we can
forecast with the added knowledge that it is highly probable that the
fifth wave will terminate at or below the upper trend channel.

As mentioned, the extended wave pattern which comprises nine sub-
waves of relatively equal dimensions is a rare occurrence. Just the same,
it is worth anticipating and watching out for. This type of extension
will usually occur in the third wave when a third wave becomes
extended. It will rarely, if ever, occur in a fifth wave.

Extensions in a Bull Market are indicative of added strength in subsequent movements. When an extension occurs at the earlier stages one can anticipate sub-normal corrective waves and a Bull move likely to reach the maximum target objectives. When extensions occur in downward impulse waves (these would be waves 1, 3, or 5 of an "A" wave or waves 1, 3, or 5 of a "C" wave) a generally weak market is anticipated. One would expect to see subsequent up waves of the next higher degree experiencing repeated "failures", falling short of the upper limits of the trend channel. One would not anticipate extensions occurring in any of the impulse moves of the upward waves should such extensions occur during the impulse moves in the downward waves.

EXTENSIONS OF EXTENSIONS

The rules govern both extensions, and extensions of extensions, which latter is not an uncommon phenomenon when a fifth wave begins to extend and span upwards. The illustrations below (Figure 23) show three different types of extension and the standard. The channels that have been drawn represent extensions of a previous fifth wave. Note the increase in the angle of incidence when an extension of an extension occurs. This is a normal phenomenon in extremely vigorous markets. Naturally one must apply the concept of extensions to wave movements to waves in all degrees.

FIGURE 23

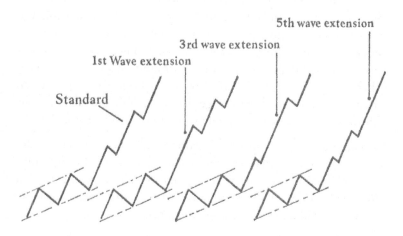

RETRACEMENTS AND DOUBLE RETRACEMENTS

When an extension occurs in the fifth wave of a movement an extremely important phenomenon will occur. In view of the relative importance of this phenomenon and its persistency, recognition of fifth wave extensions is paramount.

According to the basic tenets of the Wave Principle, most fifth wave extensions are followed by a "double retracement", such "double retracements" being reserved for extended fifth waves, never occurring during extensions that appear in first or third impulse moves.

In essence an extension of the fifth wave is never the end of a cyclical movement of that particular degree. When an extension occurs in the fifth wave, rather than anticipating the normal "A", "B, "C" down wave, characterised by a completed five-wave progression under normal circumstances, an entirely different pattern is anticipated. The practical importance of this rule of "double retracement" is that it gives the analyst a clue as to what is likely to happen next.

In *The Wave Principle* Elliott defines a retracement as "the travel of a described movement between two specified points which is covered again". A corrective down wave and subsequent resumption of the trend would therefore represent a "double retracement".

Following an extended fifth wave, the first retracement will occur immediately in a succession of three down waves, terminating approximately at the same level at which the extension began, which should also be in the vicinity of the second wave of the extension.

The second retracement will occur in the usual progress of the market and travel beyond the peak of the original extension. While the first retracement will occur immediately and in three waves, as often as not, it will take time for the second retracement to develop. However, this tendency is one of the most persistent of all the tenets of Elliott. When an extended fifth wave develops there is an exceptionally high probability that the market will ultimately rise to a new high during the second retracement of the move. Figure 24 illustrates the behaviour pattern.

FIGURE 24

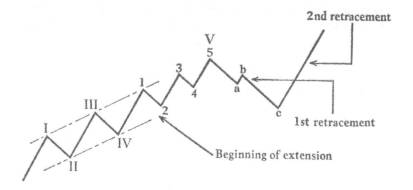

One may suddenly detect a most confusing and serious flaw in the behaviour pattern. Suddenly we find two extra waves formed by the "double retracement" which do not appear to have a place within the normal Wave Count. In the progression of a cycle one should find three impulse waves going upward interrupted by two downward corrective waves, totalling five. We should then find two downward impulse waves, interrupted by one upward corrective wave totalling three, and thus completing the eight-wave cycle. What happens to the two waves formed by the "double retracement"? How do they fit in?

Elliott made it quite clear that these "double retracements" would later fit into conventional overall patterns, i.e. it certainly would not be a question of getting a couple of extra patterns which could conveniently be added as a sort of hiatus between two sets of waves – for instance – to be disregarded with the Wave Count starting anew, after the "double retracement" and treating the next set of waves as if the "double retracement" had no meaning. Conventional wave patterns were intended to remain.

The manner in which subsequent patterns develop from the "double retracement" is quite simple and also tends to serve as a guide towards future market behaviour following a "double retracement".

When a "double retracement" occurs following the fifth wave of either the first impulse move in a series or the third impulse move in a series, normal corrective action follows. In terms of the Wave Count, the first retracement ("A", "B", "C") merely becomes Wave 2 (if following an extended first wave), or Wave 4 (if following an extension of the third wave). The second retracement merely reinstates the direction of the main trend forming the initial stages of either the third or fifth wave, remaining a part of the conventional Wave Count. In effect, the "double retracement" following an extended first or third wave merely represents a corrective wave plus part of a subsequent impulse wave.

DOUBLE RETRACEMENT AND THE EXTENDED FIFTH WAVE

The treatment of a "double retracement" following the extended fifth wave of an important movement is an entirely different state of affairs. As we know, when a movement has been completed we then expect a corrective phase which will act to purge the market of the excess developed during the preceding five-wave count. Since a "double retracement" consists of a down wave which merely acts to interrupt the overriding trend, obviously different treatment must be given when such a trend reaches its terminal state, for the subsequent down move is likely to be greater than anything experienced in that particular trend up until the terminal peak. The first retracement in a "double retracement" is only intended to equal the amplitude of the extended wave. Therefore, any "double retracement" acting as a precursor to a major down move is likely to take on a totally different meaning.

In actuality, a "double retracement" which follows an extended fifth wave forms part of an "irregular top". I will deal with this subject in greater detail as we continue but for the time being an "irregular top" should be defined as an "A", "B", "C", correction wherein the "B" wave rises to a level above the peak of the preceding Wave 5. Thus when dealing with a "double retracement" which acts as part of a terminal ending, the first retracement becomes an "A" wave rather than a complete "A", "B", "C" wave in itself. The second retracement is treated as a "B" wave rather than as the initial swing of a subsequent up move. This is then followed by a "C" wave of five waves downward.

When we have an "irregular top" of this nature, comprising a sub-normal "A" wave and stronger than usual "B" wave, the "C" wave is likely to take on quite dramatic proportions and be exceptionally fast moving. The "Great Crash" in Wall Street actually behaved in this manner.

The illustration (Figure 25) is that of the debacle known as the "Great Crash" as represented by the movement of the Dow-Jones Industrial Averages during the period November 1928 to July 1932. During my previous discussions of this period many may have been confused by my reference to the "orthodox top" which began in 1928 presaging the collapse. The chart illustrates this more clearly. The orthodox top of the 1921-8 Bull Market ended during November 1928, at which point the actual Bear Market started. Down wave "A" was actually the first wave of the Bear Market although the Dow-Jones Industrials subsequently rose to a new high at "B". The "B" wave represents the corrective wave in the Bear Market which took place between November 1928 and September 1929 thus forming an "irregular correction". The "C" wave was of extraordinary dimensions, encompassing the move from September 1929-July 1932, thus completing the "irregular correction". This move was certainly not illogical in view of the inflationary pressure built into the succeeding Bull move, the sub-normal Bear Markets that characterised the entire 1921-8 period and the extended nature of the fifth wave which terminated the entire Bull swing. Upon such a termination, corrective waves "A" and "B" were also sub-normal. Despite the fact that one Harvard professor stated in 1929, "The stock market has reached a permanently high plateau", a severe Bear Market was on the cards and already underway.

FIGURE 25: THE WALL STREET CRASH, NOVEMBER 1928-JULY 1932

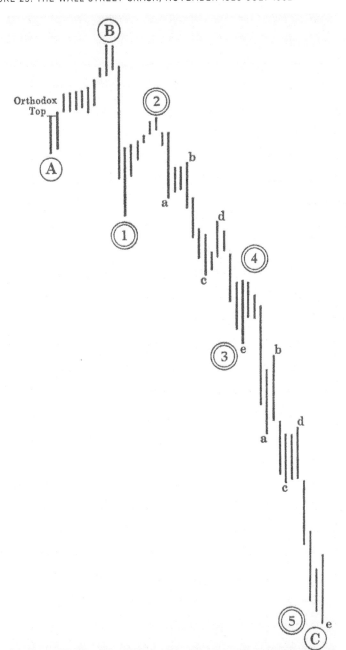

Nine:

Incorrigible Behaviour

"One of the interesting facets to Elliott's Wave Principle is the fact that the whole concept is one of GROWTH. The main direction can be considered as always upward, the downward waves always being corrections."

A. Hamilton Bolton

ORIGINALLY IT WAS intended that the title of this chapter would be "Corrective Behaviour". In view of what follows I decided the above title would better describe the contents! Up until now the main concentration has been on analysing the behaviour patterns of the impulse waves travelling in the direction of the main movement. To many inexperienced students this could well have been a mind-boggling exercise. For those who have not yet mastered this aspect of the Wave Principle, a re-reading of the previous eight chapters is recommended. However, if you've managed to get this far and still have your wits about you, by all means continue.

Just as the secondary corrections noted by Charles Dow in his work are the most descriptive aspects of market behaviour, so too are the corrective waves II and IV of the Elliott Wave Principle. I will do my best to simplify the matter by going back to basics.

A complete market cycle consists of eight waves, the overall cycle representing growth. The final three waves of the cycle are the downward corrective waves which should terminate at a level higher than the first wave of the cycle which is being corrected. Thus the net growth of a cycle after it has been completed should be *at least* equivalent to the distance covered by the first wave of the cycle.

The growth phase of the cycle comprises five waves, three of which are upward impulse waves and two of which are downward corrective waves. The upward impulse waves can be broken down into five-wave patterns of the next lower degree whereas the downward corrective waves are broken down into three waves of a lesser degree. When the five-wave growth portion of the cycle is complete we then enter the corrective phase of the cycle.

The corrective phase of the cycle normally contains three waves of the same degree as the growth phase of the cycle. The corrective waves are customarily labelled "A", "B", "C". When these waves are broken down to the next lower degree, the "A" wave will normally have five waves, the "B" wave three waves and the "C" wave five waves. The following diagram (Figure 26) shows a complete cycle with a breakdown of all components to one degree lower.

FIGURE 26

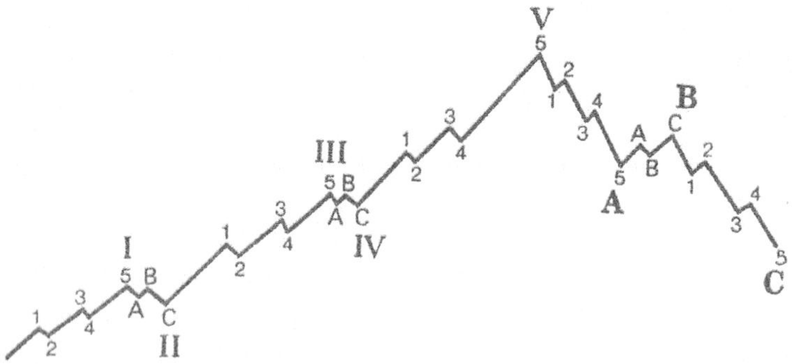

In a down wave, when the components are broken down, Waves I, III and V of the "A" Wave become impulse waves, the upward "B" Wave is a corrective wave having three components, and the downward "C" Wave has five components with Waves I, III and V the impulse waves.

If we were to break the patterns down to a degree lower still, it would be found that corrective Waves II and IV of the growth phase of the cycle will also have components of the 5-3-5 variety. Our eight-wave cycle is thus broken down into a twenty-one wave growth phase and a thirteen wave corrective phase. It is from this point that we depart.

EXTENSIONS IN THE CORRECTIVE PHASE

As discussed in the previous chapter, when dealing with the impulse waves of a cycle the departure from the basic Elliott pattern comes in the form of extended waves. While the normal Wave Count involves a series of five waves to complete the impulse phase of a cycle, either Waves 1, 3 or 5 can be extended, producing a count of nine.

When dealing with the corrective phase of a cycle the refinements which Elliott developed produce even greater departures. The corrective phase of the cycle of any degree produces what may appear as inconsistencies in the basic Wave Principle. However, when this aspect of the Wave Principle is mastered it will be readily seen how these departures give the Wave Principle its inherent flexibility rendering it that much more adaptable to stock market behaviour in the real world.

Basically, every corrective phase of a cycle will be composed of three waves. The confusion will occur when attempts are made to break these waves down into smaller components. For the sake of simplicity, first I will deal with the broad formations and then introduce the minor components.

Corrective patterns are consistent regardless of their direction or size. In an upward impulse movement, the corrective waves take the form of downward or sideways movements. In a downward impulse movement the corrective phase will produce an upward or sideways action. The corrective patterns that are to be introduced will be categorised as pertaining to either the corrective phase of a Bull swing or a Bear swing. Corrective patterns in a down move will be "inverted". Therefore, whenever the expression "inverted" appears, it should be treated as being applicable to an upward corrective phase in a downward movement.

Corrections fall into four general formations but, in action, it will sometimes be found difficult to forecast the exact pattern and extent. The important aspect of proper assessment of corrective waves is the information they will provide regarding the subsequent strength or weakness of the impulse wave that follows.

CORRECTIVE WAVE FORMATIONS – "ZIGZAG"

The patterns in Figure 27 reveal the general shape of corrective phases that will often be found in the smaller waves, particularly those seen when plotting hourly movements on the chart. It is when these corrective phases are acting within larger cycle formations that the individual components will begin to take on movements which appear to vary from the normal Wave Count. It should be noted that the general outline of the pattern will be the same regardless of the wave degree. It is only the inner components that may become subject to variation.

The simplest of all corrective waves is the "Zigzag". This particular formation provides an ideal model to which other corrective waves can be related. The "Zigzag" merely consists of a downward drive; then a rally whose proportions should be no more than two-thirds of the original downward drive. The final downward drive would approximate the proportions of the first downward drive.

FIGURE 27

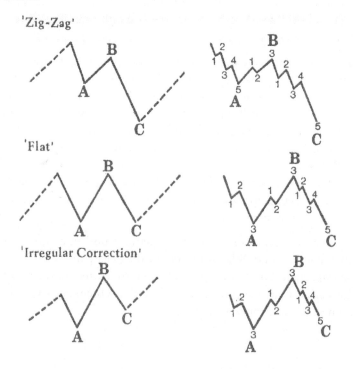

After the completion of a fifth and final wave of a major cycle degree, spanning a period of say 2-3 years, the corrective down wave will begin. If this corrective down wave takes the form of a "Zigzag", it can then be broken down into its intermediate cycle components. Accordingly, the breakdown would appear as follows (Figure 28).

FIGURE 28

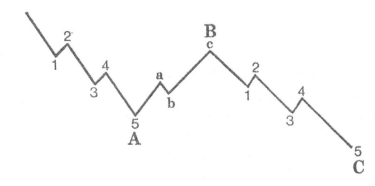

As can be seen, the breakdown is of the 5-3-5 variety. The intermediate trend of the market is downward. The components of wave "A" thus have downward impulse waves. The "B" wave is a move which is counter to the intermediate trend of the market and is thus treated as a wave which is corrective to the dominant trend of the next higher degree. In this instance the "B" wave takes the form of an "inverted zigzag". If we were to break the "inverted zigzag" down into its components of the next lower degree, the 5-3-5 count would appear again. It should be noted, however, that sub-waves of minor waves do not always sub-divide or, if they do, the time element is so small that the divisions may not be too apparent. As mentioned earlier, the "Stockmaster", a device available for tracking the minute by minute movements of the Dow-Jones Industrial Averages will go a long way towards assisting analysts in minor wave classifications under Elliott's tenets. Since this machine reproduces every single change in the movement of the Dow-Jones Industrial Averages, every single wave can be studied down to the smallest degree. The most sensitive chart that can be constructed on the movements of the London Stock Exchange is that of hourly movements, so, when dealing with the Wave

Principle in the U.K., there are likely to be many minute movements of the F.T.30 taking place on an inter-hour basis which will never be recorded. In this respect one must use some license when attempting to analyse waves of sub-minor, minuette or sub-minuette categories.

In forecasting, the characteristics of the "Zigzag" can often help the analyst to determine at what level a particular corrective phase is likely to terminate, once the first and second waves of the "A" wave have been completed.

MAXIMUM CORRECTIVE ACTION

There are two rules that will help us to determine the maximum extent of any corrective action even before the aforementioned waves have been completed:

1. If the "Zigzag" is a "4" wave of the cycle, the *maximum extent* of the corrective action will be down to the peak of wave "1" of the same cycle. At this point I would remind the reader that assessing maximum extent is not intended to suggest the move will in fact reach its maximum extent, an error made by many chartists who insist on making predictions. Maximum extent means just that. The corrective wave *may* reach its maximum extent but then again it may not. This tenet of the Wave Principle becomes useful in so far as, should the move be approaching its level of "maximum extent", the probabilities for success are highly favourable. Until such time as the move reaches its maximum extent level, the probabilities for an important turn are not quite as favourable, but this does *not* mean that an end to the corrective phase cannot occur well above the "maximum extent" level that is forecast.

The Bear Market of 1972-5 in London was the "C" wave of an "irregular top" which began in 1969. The 1969-75 formation in itself was the "IV" wave of a cycle that began in 1932. The top of Wave I of the 1932-69 cycle ended precisely at F.T.30 146. Given the tremendous power of the down move and the size of the cycle which this down move was correcting, the probabilities for success at F.T.30 146 in

January 1975 were probably about the most favourable one could ever hope for.

2. If the "Zigzag" is Wave 2 of the cycle, the maximum extent of the down move will be down to Wave I of the cycle of *the next lower degree*. As we have learned, when the first waves of a new Bull move are completed, we will then experience a down wave of longer time and greater amplitude than either of the two corrective waves that appeared in the succeeding five wave movement. This wave will become Wave 2 of the next higher degree. Therefore we can establish a minimum and maximum expectancy for the succeeding corrective movement. The minimum expectancy would be equal to the maximum time period of either Wave 2 or Wave 4 of the preceding movement. The minimum amplitude will also be equal to the maximum amplitude of either Wave 2 or Wave 4 of the succeeding movement. Let us use the following five wave sequence as an example (Figure 29).

FIGURE 29

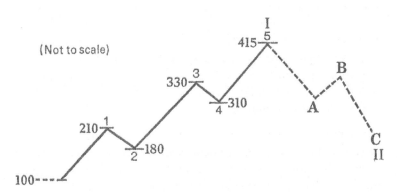

(Not to scale)

Wave I – 110 Points over 5 months
Wave 2 – 30 Points over 2 months
Wave 3 – 150 Points over 8 months
Wave 4 – 20 Points over 3 months
Wave 5 – 105 Points over 5 months

In Figure 29 we have a sequence of five waves showing their time span and amplitude. When attempting to establish the *minimum expectancy* for the amplitude of the II Wave ("A", "B", "C" corrective "Zigzag") we determine the maximum amplitude of either Wave 2 or Wave 4. In this case the maximum amplitude was the 2 Wave involving a down swing of 30 points. The minimum periodicity of the down move can be established by determining the maximum periodicity of either the 2 Wave or the 4 Wave. In this respect the 4 Wave was the longer wave in time involving a down swing lasting 3 months. Thus we can establish the minimum expectancy of Wave II which will act to correct the five wave movement as involving a minimum fall of 30 points over a minimum period of 3 months. Simply, the basic tenet of Elliott states that the corrective wave following five completed waves of a cycle must be greater in time and amplitude than any of the previous corrective waves of the cycle, which, when completed, will become a wave in the cycle of the next higher degree.

When determining the maximum extent of the subsequent Wave II, we merely establish where the peak of the first impulse wave of the next lower degree of Wave I occurred. In the above instance, such a peak occurred at 210. In order to establish the maximum periodicity of the move we revert to the "Golden Ratio" of the Fibonacci Summation Series. The time span of the corrective wave should not be greater than 0.618 of the time span of the wave which it is correcting. In Figure 29, the total five-wave formation spanned 23 months. The maximum expectancy for the corrective move would thus be approximately 14 months.

As you can see, even before we begin the corrective phase of the cycle we can obtain some rough guidelines as to what can be expected in terms of the subsequent magnitude of the coming Bear phase. In the example in Figure 29 we established a minimum expectation of the next down move as being not less than 30 points spanning a period of not less than 3 months, and having a maximum expectancy of 14 months spanning no more than 205 points.

USE IN INVESTMENT STRATEGY

At this stage many who attempt to make predictions with their charts will dismiss the idea as offering a margin of error which is too broad. This is because most fail to recognise that the margin of error implicit in most chart work is either much broader or totally irrelevant, the latter being the thesis of students of modern capital market theory. When dealing with factors which tend to anticipate events before they occur rather than following them as they occur, movements of minimum and maximum expectancy which provide empirical evidence of resolution to the extent which Elliott has provided, can be of immense benefit to the investor in terms of overall strategy. In the preceding example, investors would have liquidated their holdings upon the completion of the five-wave movement. One would not consider any repurchases until the down move had lasted at least 3 months and involved a minimum down swing of 30 points. Should the down move go into its thirteenth month and involve a swing of say 190 points, investors would then start picking the shares they intended to buy for the succeeding up swing in anticipation of a big bull move soon to develop.

Naturally, the question will arise, "What does one do in the intervening 11 months?" Should the market turn upward after the fourth month and one waited for a further nine months to take action, a massive move could have been completed. The answer to that question comes from the inherent behaviour pattern of the "Zigzag".

By the time the down move has reached its minimum expectancy based on the calculations that were made by analysing the structure of the five-wave up-move, we will no doubt have a great deal more data to help us. For instance, once waves 1 and 2 of the "A" wave of the "Zigzag" have developed, we can employ the channelling technique described previously. We could then determine the probable amplitude and periodicity of the "A" wave from which we can obtain a further probability as to the extent of both the "B" wave and the "C" wave. In development of a "Zigzag" the "B" wave will be shorter in time and amplitude than the "A" wave, while the "C" wave will approximate the "A" wave both in time and amplitude.

When waves 1 and 2 of the corrective "A" wave have been completed we would thus carry out the following procedure:

1. A channel will be constructed in accordance with the principles outlined. Guidelines will then be established for the duration and amplitude of the completed five Waves which will comprise Wave "A" of the "Zigzag". We can then establish a minimum amplitudinal expectancy for the "B" wave.

2. The minimum expectancy of the "B" wave can be established by assessing the maximum duration and amplitude of Waves 2 and 4 of the five waves that comprise the "A" wave as established by the channel. Remember Elliott's rule regarding extensions. Extensions are unlikely to occur in corrective waves. Therefore neither the "A" wave, the "B" wave, nor the "C" wave are likely to be subject to any extended movements.

3. The maximum expectancy of the "B" wave can be established by treating the bottom of Wave 1 as the maximum point of corrective action, and by multiplying the time span of the "A" wave by the "Golden Ratio" of 0.618 in order to determine the maximum time it will take to complete the move.

4. Once a probable minimum and maximum time and amplitudinal expectation has been calculated for the "B" wave, one merely adds the expected amplitude of the "A" wave to the peak of the "B" wave to get an approximate idea of what the total "A" "B" "C" correction is likely to involve. The time span can be calculated in a like manner. The time span of the "C" wave should approximate that of the "A" wave.

5. A further refinement is brought into play when we near the terminal juncture of the pattern. Once the "A" and "B" waves have been completed and followed by four waves of the "C" wave, we can pin-point the exact ending of the down move by using a further tenet of Elliott. Regardless of the nature of the corrective action, there is an extraordinarily high probability that Wave 5 of the "C" wave will be equal to Wave 1 of that same "C" wave. By adding the amplitude of Wave 1 of the "C" wave to the peak of Wave 4 we will thus come up with the exact bottom of the "A" "B" "C" move.

FURTHER CORRECTIVE WAVE FORMATIONS

Forecasting the extent of corrective waves would be a simple matter if all of these corrective waves took the form of the simple Elliott "Zigzag". Unfortunately they do not. However, as we develop the more complex wave formations one should not be overly dismayed, because many of the principles governing the behaviour characteristics of the "Zigzag" also apply to other corrective waves regardless of their composition. For example, Elliott's rule governing Waves 1 and 5 of the "C" wave apply to not only the "Zigzag" but also the "Flat" and the "Irregular Correction" as shown in Figure 27. The main difference between the three corrections will be the count of the component sub-waves. The only types of corrections where this rule would not apply would be in the "Complex Correction", "Mixed Complex Correction", "Triangles" and "Horizontals" this latter category being quite rare.

The rules governing minimum and maximum amplitude, and minimum and maximum time spans of the corrective waves apply to every type of corrective wave. While it will often prove difficult to determine what type of corrective action will subsequently take place, one can still be comforted by the knowledge that regardless of the irregularities of the corrective action, its maximum extent in time and amplitude will be governed by the relationships outlined. The same holds true for the minimum time and amplitude expectations.

Elliott has gone into great detail categorising the various forms of corrective action in order to produce a greater degree of accuracy, such accuracy often uncalled for. In any event, it is wise to make an attempt at categorising every type of corrective action as it occurs, if only to cross-check the broad guidelines that may have previously been forecast.

THE "FLAT"

Obviously, the "Flat" takes its name from its appearance. Whereas the "Zigzag" is composed of a sharp downward drive, a rally that retraces all but one of the five sub-minor components, then another downward drive of similar dimensions to the first downward drive, the "Flat" takes on much stronger properties. The "B" wave of a "Flat" will often rally to the peak of the five wave pattern which it is correcting. This would mean the "C" wave, usually of similar dimensions to the "A" wave, would terminate at approximately the same level as the "A" wave. In this respect, the peak of the "Flat" is often at the same level as the peak of the previous Bull phase (or trough of the Bear phase in the event of an "inverted flat"), while the two troughs of the "Flat" are unlikely to be in close proximity.

The most important distinction of the "Flat" for forecasting purposes is the difference in the component minor wave structure. Broadly, the "Flat" will appear as in Figure 27. When broken down into the component waves of the next lower degree, instead of comprising five waves downward, three upward and five downward, as in the case of the "Zigzag", the "Flat" will produce a count of three waves downward, three waves upward, and five waves downward. Figure 30 is an example of the "Flat" broken down into waves of two lower degrees.

"Flats" are rarely perfectly horizontal. In either an up trend or a down trend, the corrective "Flat" will be sloping gently upward or downward. What gives the "Flat" its characteristic is the close proximity of the "B" wave to the peak (or trough if "inverted") of the five-wave pattern which it is correcting and the reasonably close proximity of the point of the "C" wave to the terminal point of the "A" wave.

In the following chapter you will learn how "Flats" and "Zigzags" often alternate in accordance with Elliott's "theory of alternation". One will find that normally, the corrective 2-Wave of a five-wave pattern will be a "Zigzag", while the corrective 4-Wave will be a "Flat". If the corrective 2-Wave was a "Flat" one would then anticipate a "Zigzag" as the corrective 4-Wave.

FIGURE 30

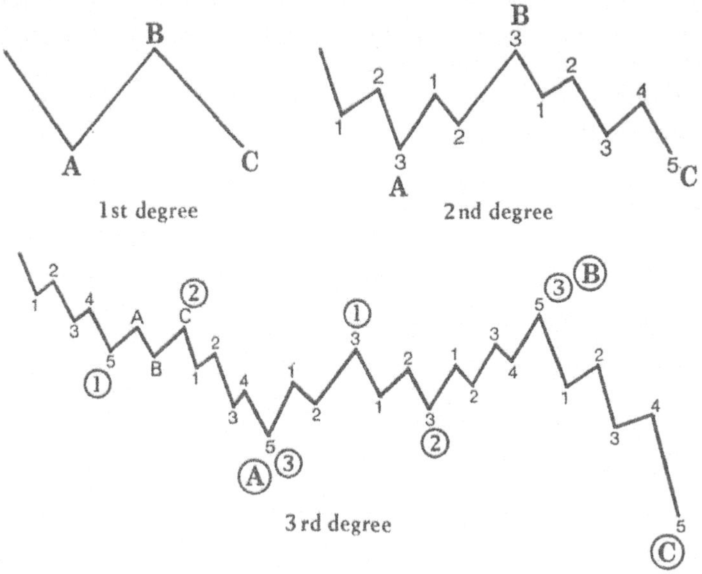

1st degree

2nd degree

3rd degree

Once we have completed three waves of a five-wave pattern and the 2-Wave has been assessed as a "Zigzag" we will alter our forecasting techniques when trying to establish the dimensions of the corrective downwave IV. As mentioned, the components of the "A" wave of the "Flat" will only produce two down swings interrupted by an up swing giving a total count of three waves. Since the complete count will only be three waves, we are unable to use the channelling technique designed for five-wave movements as was the case of the "Zigzag". Thus when projecting the extent of the "A" wave of a "Flat" we must deal with movements of the degree lower, treating the "A" wave of the "Flat" as a separate "Zigzag" in smaller form.

If we break the "Flat" down into its components of two degrees lower, we find the "A" wave consists of a "Zigzag", which in turn consists of a downward movement having five waves, an upward movement having three waves and a downward movement of five waves. The "B" wave of the "Flat" takes the form of an "inverted zigzag" which, broken down, will have five upward waves of the next lower degree, three downward waves of the next lower degree and five upward waves of the next lower degree. The "C" wave of the "Flat" will have the same components as any other "C" wave, i.e. three waves down interrupted by two waves up. When broken down the normal 5-3-5-3-5 count will tie in with the breakdown of the "A" and "B" waves as in the following illustration (Figure 31).

FIGURE 31. BREAKDOWN OF THE FLAT

When waves 1 and 2 of Wave① of the "A" wave have been completed, we then draw our channel in the same manner as we would do for any "Zigzag". This channel will then give us the approximate terminal level for Wave① of wave "A" of the "Flat". We then use the same procedure outlined with respect to plotting the terminal ending for the "B" wave and the "C" wave of the "Zigzag" to give us waves 2 and 3 of the "Flat", which in turn provides the terminal point of wave "A" of the "Flat". Once the terminal point of wave "A" of the "Flat" has been calculated the rest is comparatively simple for both the "B" wave and the "C" wave of the "Flat" approximate the same dimensions as the "A" wave.

There are several aids that will help when dealing with the "Flat". The first aspect one must consider is the minimum expectancy of the projected corrective move. Basically, the "Flat" is composed of a downward "Zigzag" followed by an upward "Zigzag", then a normal five-wave downward move. Should a relatively shallow downward "Zigzag" have been completed in less time than we would normally expect for the completion of a "Zigzag", it is likely that such a downward move is only part of a much larger corrective pattern, not complete in itself. One would then be placed on the alert for the possible development of a "Flat". Naturally, should such a downward move take place in a 4-Wave, the previous corrective 2-Wave having been a "Zigzag", all the more reason to be on the alert for the "Flat".

At times, the "C" wave of a "Flat" will take on added dimensions. This is another tenet dealt with in detail under Elliott's "Theory of Alternation". One will be warned of such an occurrence when the first wave of the "C" wave falls below Wave 2 of the "B" wave yet is significantly higher than the beginning of the "B" wave as in the following diagram (Figure 32). (Note: For purposes of illustration the "C" wave has been broken down into one degree lower than the "A" wave and the "B" wave.)

FIGURE 32. ELONGATED "C WAVE"

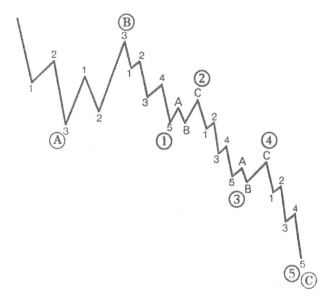

When this occurs one must revise the projection downward. Whereas originally it would have been anticipated that the "C" wave of the "Flat" would have terminated at or about the level of the "A" wave, when the first wave of the "C" wave penetrates the bottom of Wave 2

of the "B" wave we readjust our minimum expectation for this "C" wave in the same manner as discussed when attempting to anticipate the terminal point of a "C" wave in dealing with the "Zigzag".

Further, when attempting to forecast the bottom of the "C" wave of a "Flat" one assumes Wave 3 will be of greater dimensions than Wave 1, and Wave 5 will approximate Wave 1. Thus we multiply Wave 1 by three, then subtract the anticipated maximum expectancy of the corrective moves as previously outlined. The result will give us the expected dimension of the "C" wave when the first wave of such a "C" wave takes on a greater than anticipated amplitude. One can use the channelling technique or any of the other methods which enable one to forecast the terminal point of a five-wave movement. Elliott makes special note of this phenomenon in *Nature's Law*, thus: "Whether or not Wave "C" of an inverted "Flat" is elongated or not, it still remains corrective."

"IRREGULAR CORRECTIONS"

When the "B" wave of a corrective movement exceeds the peak of the fifth wave of a cycle which it is correcting, this is defined as an "Irregular Correction" under the tenets of Elliott's treatment of corrective waves. The fifth wave of the cycle is considered the "orthodox top", while the "B" wave of the corrective phase which follows is considered an "irregular top". The count for the "Irregular Correction" is the same as that of the "Flat"; the "A" wave comprises two downward movements interspersed by a counter upward movement, the "B" wave is comprised of two upward moves interrupted by one downward movement, and the "C" wave consists of three downward waves interrupted by two upward waves, as is the normal characteristic of the "C" wave in the "Zigzag" and the "Flat".

Figure 33 shows a normal five-wave progression followed by an "Irregular Correction". Note the position of the "orthodox top". Waves "A", "B" and "C" all constitute *one* correction, notwithstanding the fact that the end of Wave "B" may be higher than Wave V.

FIGURE 33

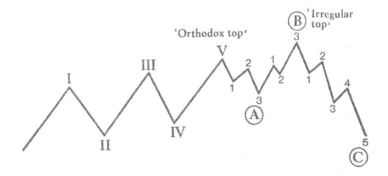

Actually, the "Irregular Correction" is probably the simplest of all corrective patterns to deal with because of its habitual occurrence following an extended five-wave pattern. Although the "Irregular Correction" sometimes appears following a normal five-wave upward movement, it most frequently appears following an extended fifth wave. The "A" wave of the "Irregular Correction" can be simply established, since it is the first retracement which follows an extension. Since such a retracement only covers the ground of the extended wave, the "A" wave of the "Irregular Correction" can be easily ascertained as terminating at the precise level at which the extension began. We can establish a minimum expectancy for the "B" wave of the "Irregular Correction" since we know the extended wave will be doubly retraced. The "B" wave of the "Irregular Correction" will thus reach a level at least as high as the peak of extended Wave V. It should be noted that "Irregular Corrections" do not follow extended fifth waves on all occasions. Sometimes an extended fifth wave will merely be followed by a "Zigzag". The factor of periodicity should be the final arbiter in this respect. When the first retracement which follows the extended waves takes place over a period of time which is less than the minimum expectancy for the correction, one can assume an "Irregular Correction" is in the course of development. Should the first retracement be protracted in time, encompassing a periodicity greater than that of the longest corrective wave of the cycle which is being corrected, it is then likely that the first retracement will take the form of a normal "Zigzag", retracing the extended wave. The second retracement will actually constitute a wave in the main trend rather than the "B" wave of a "double retracement".

"Irregular Corrections" also occur during normal unextended five-wave movements. As mentioned previously, the 1969-75 movement produced an "Irregular Correction". The "orthodox top" was in January of 1969. The "A" wave took the F.T.30 down from 520 to 305 between January 1969 and March of 1971. The "B" wave of the movement took the F.T.30 to a level higher than the "orthodox top" to F.T.30 545. Elliott cites the "Great Crash" as providing an excellent model. The "orthodox top" took place in November 1928 preceding the "irregular top" which subsequently developed a massive elongated "C" wave, the latter being characteristic of both the "Flat" and the "Irregular Correction".

The diagram (Figure 34) shows an "Irregular Correction" following an extended fifth wave, and also following a normal fifth wave.

FIGURE 34. (1) AN IRREGULAR CORRECTION A, B, C, FOLLOWING AN EXTENDED FIFTH WAVE.
(2) AN IRREGULAR CORRECTION A, B, C, FOLLOWING A NORMAL FIFTH WAVE

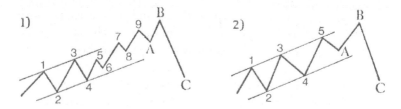

Rules for forecasting the minimum and maximum extent of "Irregular Corrections" are the same as noted for the "Zigzag" and the "Flat" with the exception of those items peculiar to the "Irregular Correction". When dealing with corrective waves generally, some broad observations should be noted. As a general proposition, waves along the main trend composed of 5 sub-waves (or 9 in the case of an extension) will prove to be far more easily identifiable than will be the corrective waves. Corrective waves, particularly in bull cycles, tend to develop irregularities and, as we have discovered, may not necessarily be 3-wave affairs or subject to the normal 5-3-5 count.

It follows then, if a wave cannot be sub-divided into five sub-waves according to Elliott's tenets, it therefore must be a corrective wave. In analysing the corrective waves, far more latitude is allowed than in the case of the more readily definable impulse waves, when making a count. By their very nature, impulse waves tend to be clean-cut affairs, as if these waves were generated by sudden impulse behaviour. Impulse waves are usually so well delineated that it is almost impossible for even the novice to misinterpret them. Like the perfect play in billiards – so easy that it keeps the duffer's interest up!

Ten:

"Double Threes", "Triple Threes", "Horizontals", "Triangles"... and all that!

"By extrusion, we match the heartbeats of today's and yesterday's markets."

William C. Garrett

A. HAMILTON BOLTON, in his work, *The Elliott Wave Principle*, probably did more to clarify some of the more obscure facets of Elliott's work than any other analyst who has ever studied these principles. Most analysts have always found the subject of corrective action to be the most elusive and it is in this area that Bolton's work was exceedingly valuable.

In his dissertation on corrective action, Bolton begins with the basic premise that a five-wave movement in the direction of the main trend is followed by a correction. Deductive logic therefore would state that a Bull Market cannot consist of three waves, it must consist of five waves. Thus if one finds a three-wave upward pattern of sufficient size to qualify as a Bull Market – as for instance the Bull move which began in March 1971 in London, terminating in May of 1971 – then this is not a Bull Market as such, but really two Bull Markets. These two Bull Markets would actually constitute part of a correction within a correction. In the particular instance noted, the two intermediate term Bull Markets of the March 1971-May 1972 move in London were actually the "B" wave of cycle Wave IV, whose "C" wave produced one of the worst Bear Markets in the history of the London Stock Exchange. Ironically, the component structure of the move prior to the development of the "C" wave was astonishingly similar to the "irregular top" which presaged the "Great Crash" in Wall Street.

The entire affair may reek of pure semantics but the concept goes far beyond. We must continually think in terms of Elliott's approach to the movement of capital markets.

The market move in London from March 1971 to May 1972 may have produced the rewards that Bull Markets usually produce, but there were ominous overtones about the whole affair, particularly when one considers the structure of the preceding Bear Market movement from January 1969 to March 1971. Just as Bull Markets will always be composed of five waves, Bear Markets are composed of three waves. Therefore one may think of the 1969-71 affair as a Bear Market and the 1971-2 affair as a Bull Market, but in both instances neither were of the dimensions that would assist one in further categorisation, for each was incomplete. The January 1969-March 1971 down wave that took the F.T.30 from 520 to 305 was a five-wave affair. Therefore it could not have been a complete Bear Market. The move up from March 1971 to May 1972 that took the F.T.30 from 305 to 545 was not a complete Bull Market, for it had only three waves. It took the devastating Bear Market of May 1972 to January 1975 to place the movements into perspective. Hindsight now tells us the entire move from January 1969 involved a five-wave down swing which was the "A" wave, a "double inverted zigzag" which was the "B" wave, followed by a truncated "C" wave, all combined to make an "irregular correction" which was Wave IV of a cycle move.

We focus on this point in order to introduce another of Elliott's corrective formations which deviate from the norm, this being the "double zigzag" or, as Elliott puts it in *Nature's Law*, the "double three".

This particular refinement of the Wave Principle never actually appeared in Elliott's original *Wave Principle* published in 1938, nor is it likely that he had done sufficient research in the area to discover the phenomenon at the time of his writing for *The Financial World*. This particular addendum to the Wave Principle was not introduced until the publication of his final work, *Nature's Law* in 1946. Adding to his categories of "Flats", "Zigzags" and "Irregular Corrections", Elliott introduces a series of "Complex Corrections" which would appear to complete every feasible type of wave categorisation. Elliott doesn't state the frequency of occurrence in the case of the following mutants but it is inferred that corrective waves can take on a greater number than originally suggested, notably in the case of a "Flat".

COMPLEX CORRECTIONS

In *Nature's Law* Elliott first dealt with the simple "Zigzag", demonstrating the normal characteristic down move. He compares this "Zigzag" with a "Flat". We then hit a "grey area" in his writing for he then immediately transcends to the "double sideways correction" which he claims can be composed of seven waves as in the following diagram (Figure 35).

FIGURE 35

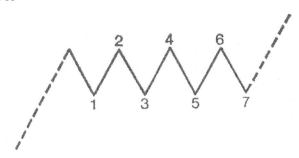

He does place a rarity value on the "triple sideways movement" as comprised of eleven waves which would appear as follows (Figure 36).

FIGURE 36

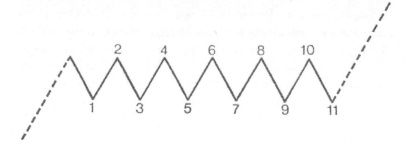

Elliott concludes his discussion on "Complex Corrective Waves" by stating:

> "In other words, a sideways correction to an up trend ends in a down trend, whether it is composed of 1, 3, 7, or 11 waves, and are named as follows:
>
> 3 waves is a 'single 3'
> 7 waves is a 'double 3'
> 11 waves is a 'triple 3' "

Presumably, the "double 3" and the "triple 3" refer to a double and triple "Flat" in case of wave characteristics resembling a "Flat". Elliott goes on to demonstrate the phenomenon relative to an inverted upward movement, and here we assume he was referring to double and triple "inverted Zigzags" which was the inference drawn by A. Hamilton Bolton, who adopted the latter terminology for these complex corrections, providing a much clearer breakdown of the "single zigzag" and the "double zigzag" than did Elliott himself.

FIGURE 37

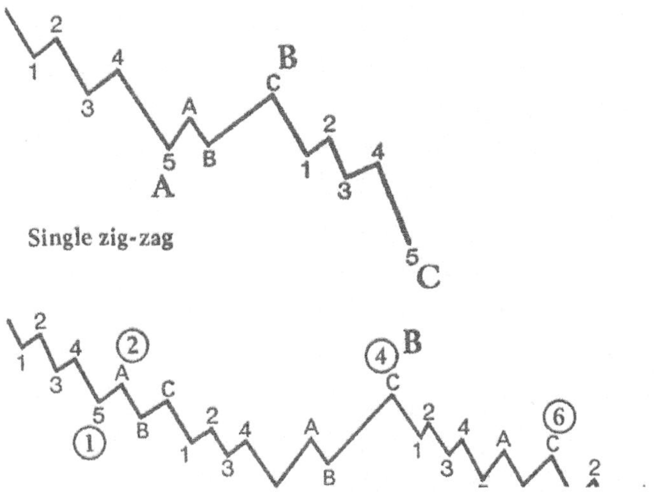

Single zig-zag

These "double" and "triple Zigzags" seem to offer an exception to the general principle that the third wave ("C" wave) of a corrective movement, up or down, always ends in a five sub-wave formation. It is the general rule of the five sub-wave ending that gives the analyst the all-important clue as to when the move is over.

Thus, with the addition of "Double Threes" and "Triple Threes", we can now enumerate the variety of corrective waves which one would be seeking:

1. "Zigzag"

2. "Double Zigzag"

3. "Triple Zigzag"

4. "Inverted Zigzag"

5. "Inverted Double Zigzag"

6. "Inverted Triple Zigzag"

7. "Flat"

8. "Double Flat"

9. "Triple Flat"

10. "Inverted Double Flat"

11. "Irregular Corrections"

12. "Inverted Irregular Corrections"

13. "Mixed Double Zigzags"

14. "Mixed Inverted Zigzags"

Items 13 and 14, would appear to be a combination of a "Zigzag", "Flats" and "Irregulars". In *Nature's Law* Elliott illustrates his "Mixed Double Threes" as in Figure 38.

FIGURE 38

'Double threes' mixed
Correcting a downtrend

Correcting an uptrend

'Double threes' mixed irregular
Correcting an uptrend

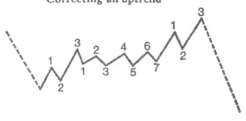

Correcting a downtrend

It will now become apparent that with this variety of corrective behaviour patterns it can become extremely difficult for any analyst to be sure what may be expected. However, generally speaking, double and triple threes and most of the "mixed" complex formations would never be seen in waves of large degrees, but only in smaller formations of sub-minor and minor dimensions. One suspects that Elliott may have been attempting to take his work a bit too far by adding to the complexity of these corrective waves, the extent of which can be established, more or less, by many of the ancillary tools inherent in the Wave Principle. As we will see, clues to future market behaviour are offered when these more complex formations are discovered. However, one wonders whether the work of discovery is commensurate with the information subsequently provided.

TRIANGLES AND HORIZONTALS

To top the whole question of corrections, we still have "Triangles" and "Horizontals" to deal with, these often occurring in larger formations.

In the case of the "Triangle" we have a further exception from the basic rule of a three-wave corrective pattern. However, in this instance, the formation is very easy to spot due to its shape and to the fact that "triangles" are fairly rare and, so far as has been discovered, will only occur as Wave 4 of the five-wave movement. They cannot appear as impulse Waves 1, 3 or 5, nor are they likely to appear as corrective Wave 2. Therefore the possibilities of making an error by incorrectly interpreting the components of a "Triangle" are negligible.

In Elliott's *Wave Principle* published in 1938, he referred to "Triangles" as being of both the contracting and expanding type. By the time he gained further experience with the *Wave Principle* he decided the only type of "Triangle" worthy of consideration was the contracting variety (Figure 39). The primary deviation from the normal three-wave corrective rule is evident in the fact that the "Triangle" is a five-wave effort comprising sub-minor waves of a three-wave variety. The count of the inner components of a "Triangle" would thus be 3-3-3-3-3, each contracting in amplitude.

FIGURE 39

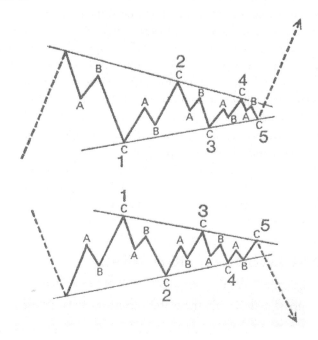

While it would not be advisable to spend too much time engaging in the mental gymnastics necessary for the interpretation of the Complex Corrections in the form of "Double Threes" and "Triple Threes" in their mixed and inverted forms, it is certainly advisable to study the principles involving the triangular formation and attempt to discover their occurrence. The empirical evidence which supports the probable resolution of a "Triangle" will prove that the time taken is well worth the potential rewards. Although rare, when a "Triangle" occurs, its subsequent resolution is extremely reliable.

As Elliott explains in his original *Wave Principle*:

> "Wave movements occasionally taper off to a point or broaden out from a point in the form of a triangle. These triangular formations are important since they indicate the direction the market will take at the conclusion or approximate apex of the triangle."

Elliott segregates "Triangles" into two classes, the "Horizontal" and "Diagonal". Elliott claims the development of a "Horizontal Triangle" represents hesitation on the part of the main price movement.

At the conclusion of the "Horizontal Triangle" when the apex is broken, the market will resume the original trend – upward or downward – that it is pursuing prior to the triangular hesitation. Horizontal triangles have the same significance as "Flats". The following (Figure 40) are examples of "Triangles", one which contracts and one which expands. The "expanding triangle" was dropped from Elliott's later work. Its inclusion at this stage is for purely academic interest. Note in the example shown the manner in which the "Triangle" comprises Wave 4 of the five-wave movement. The "Triangle" is completed at "E" and Wave 5 of the movement commences at that point.

FIGURE 40

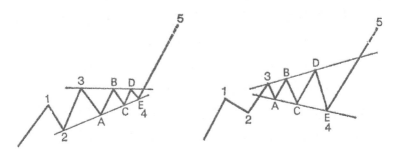

Elliott also divides "Horizontal Triangles" into four classes as they appear in Figure 41.

FIGURE 41

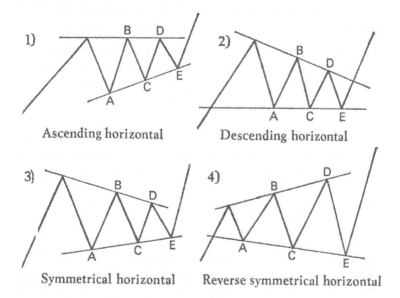

1) Ascending horizontal

2) Descending horizontal

3) Symmetrical horizontal

4) Reverse symmetrical horizontal

1. Ascending = Level peaks and rising bottoms.

2. Descending = Level bottoms and descending peaks.

3. Symmetrical = Falling peaks and rising bottoms.

4. Reversal symmetrical = Broadening from start to finish in a series of rising peaks and falling bottoms.

(Note: Since the fourth category was subsequently discarded by Elliott as being the expanding type of "Triangle" once again we include this item on academic grounds only.)

Diagonal Triangles are merely divided into two classes, the upward diagonal and the downward diagonal as follows in Figure 42.

FIGURE 42

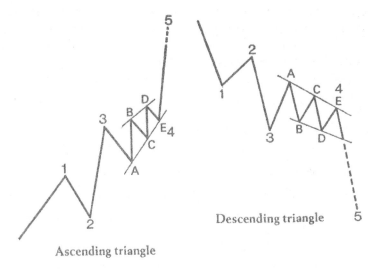

Ascending triangle

Descending triangle

Elliott claims, and this is borne out by my own experience, that "Triangles" occur only in Wave 4 formations, and whether horizontal or diagonal, contain five waves, each of which have three sub-waves. Where there are less than five waves, the "Triangle" will fall outside the Wave phenomena observable by Elliott. Such a triangular formation should then be treated as only a minor component of what is likely to be a much larger formation.

Elliott points out that the most important aspect to be noted in respect of the "Horizontal Triangle" is where it begins. The "B" wave of the "Triangle" must be "fixed" for it is the "B" wave which will dictate the subsequent direction of the market's movement. Obviously, in order to "fix" the "B" wave, establishing its peak and trough, one must be able to identify the "A" wave. In Figure 43 (a "Horizontal Triangle") the direction of the "B" wave is downward. At the conclusion of the "E" wave of the "Triangle" the market, which has been hesitating, will then resume the original decline.

In the adjoining diagram (another "Horizontal Triangle") the five-wave pattern can be seen as interrupting an upward movement. Whereas the diagram on the left refers to a move which is likely to occur as the

"4" wave of either the "A" wave or the "C" wave of a downward "Zigzag", the illustration on the right in Figure 43 is likely to occur as the "4" wave of a five-wave upward series. For the sake of illustration, one would assume the "2" wave of a five-wave series bottomed at II followed by a three-wave peak at III. What then follows is the triangular hesitation which resumes the direction of the "B" wave of the triangle.

FIGURE 43

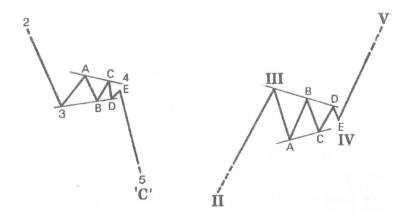

To all intents and purposes, the student can treat the "Triangle" in its various forms as a Wave 4 phenomenon, rarely occurring in any other segment of the cycle, and, even then, only occurring on infrequent occasions. However, any approach to the stock market must involve the recognition that the market can do what it likes any time it likes. In this respect, Elliott makes reference to the occasional development of a "Triangle" during the development of an "extended fifth" wave, in view of what is likely to occur when the pattern is completed. In Figure 44 one will note the orthodox top of the fifth wave, marked OT, falls short of its normal expectancy (this is defined as a "failure", a subject to be discussed in the next chapter) but then proceeds to develop an extension. Such a development could occur as a result of sudden positive news developments or other extraneous items, causing a trend which was previously in the process of weakening to suddenly develop added *temporary* strength. One would expect to see a contraction in volume during the "Triangle", well below the peak at the orthodox top of the fifth wave.

Also in Figure 44, minor Wave 2, which is the second wave of the triangle, is downward. The market can be expected to reverse its direction at the end of the upward "Diagonal Triangle", e.g. when the fifth wave of the "Triangle" has been completed. Whereas the normal expectancy for the corrective phase which follows an extended fifth wave is a "double retracement", in this instance the market has been in the process of developing weakness prior to the extended fifth wave which was a "Triangle". This "Triangle" merely adds to the excesses of the price movement, therefore, rather than anticipating a "double retracement" which would (a) pull back to the level at which the extended fifth wave began, (b) recover the ground lost and subsequently rise to a level above the extended fifth wave, we would now anticipate an "A", "B", "C" correction returning to the base of the "Triangle" (bottom of Wave IV). The "Triangle" which is characteristic of hesitation in the price action, would preclude the development of an impulse wave of the next higher degree, or a "B" wave which rises to a level above the extended fifth wave (as is the case with an "irregular correction" following an extended fifth wave) until the entire amplitude of the "Triangle" had been retraced.

FIGURE 44

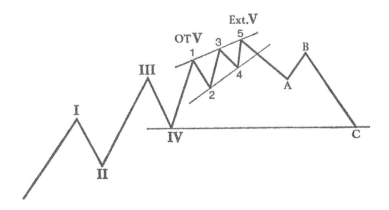

Elliott makes special note of the occurrence of a "triangular" development in the fifth wave of a primary movement, since one must then anticipate a very rapid reversal from the fifth wave terminal point. As a general rule, the only "Triangles" one will run across are the "horizontal" variety which develop as Wave IV movements. When one discovers the development of an upward or downward "Diagonal Triangle", the formation can only be treated as having reliable forecasting value when it appears as the fifth wave of an important upward or downward movement. A sharp "thrust" will follow the completion of the fifth wave of this type of "Triangle".

All the waves of a "Triangle" must be part of a movement in the same direction, either upwards, downwards or sideways. If the pattern appears "mixed", no "Triangle" is present.

When a "Triangle" appears in a large formation, spanning say, six to twelve months or longer, it will take a fully developed appearance, each of the five waves of the "Triangle" having three components as shown in Figure 39. When the formation takes place over a shorter period the fourth and fifth waves may not appear fully developed. Waves 1, 2 and 3 may take on the normal appearance of having three components, but Waves 4 and 5 may only appear as involving one move each, as appears in Figure 45. In the very small formations, spanning one day to say two weeks, the waves of the "Triangle" are often composed of singular movements as in Figure 46. The main guideline to the formation is in the outline, that is the tangents drawn on the peaks and troughs of the wave components.

FIGURE 45

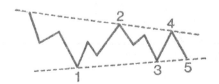

FIGURE 46

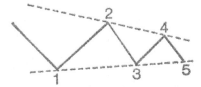

Empirically, the "Triangle" precedes a very powerful "thrust" in the direction of the "2" wave. Before taking action on such a "thrust" one must await the completion of the fifth wave of the "Triangle" in order to be sure that such a "Triangle" has been formed. Here, Elliott offers an important clue:

> "When the range (weekly or daily) in a triangle embraces the entire width of the triangle, the end has about arrived. Confirmation should be required in wave number five."

THE TENSION IN THE TRIANGLE

A most interesting analogy to the "Triangle" has been given by William L. Jiler in his book, *How Charts Can Help You in the Stock Market*:

> "When a stock fluctuates in progressively smaller price ranges, it is in effect winding up like a spring in a mechanical toy. And just as a wound spring holds enough tension to move a toy, a coiling action in a stock can propel prices. In the toy, the tension is mechanical. In the market, the tension builds on the increasing uncertainties of buyers and sellers."

Jiler notes that a "Triangle" will invariably follow an advancing or declining phase of the price action. The first upward wave of a "Triangle" will produce a rally in a Bear phase. The peak of the "Triangle" will be achieved when buying power dries up and profit taking develops. At that level a measure of uncertainty will overtake the Bulls thus causing a reaction which will complete the "B" wave of the "Triangle". The ensuing rally which is the "C" wave of the "Triangle" will upset many who feel prices are too high and that the Bear trend may not have been completed. The declining "D" wave of the "Triangle" will increase anxiety amongst the Bulls while the "E" wave will have a similar effect on the bears. Characteristic of the "Triangle" will be the fact that the volume of trading will have steadily diminished as buyers and sellers become increasingly uncertain about the future direction of share prices. At the apex of the "Triangle" buying and selling pressures reach a complete balance. At that stage it takes very little buying power or selling pressure to tip the balance and produce a strong wave of self-feeding buying or selling, thus providing the Elliott "thrust", a phenomenon which follows both the "Triangle" or any horizontal movement depicting indecisive action.

Jiler gave a weighting of 60 per cent to the probability that once a "Triangle" is resolved the direction of the trend which preceded the "Triangle" will continue, as would be the case when the "Triangle" represents the fourth wave of a five-wave movement. The balance of supply and demand is stated to be only of a temporary nature representing nothing more than a pause in the long range trend of prices. The other 40 per cent of the time, obviously in the case of an ascending or descending "Triangle" occurring as a fifth wave extension, these "Triangles" can be patterns which presage a major reversal.

This chapter concludes our study of the most complex aspect of the Wave Principle, Elliott's treatment of the corrective waves. We have seen how the impulse waves are easily definable while the corrective waves can take many shapes and forms. Probably the most troublesome aspect of the corrective phase of a market movement is that there is no way of telling what type of correction will ultimately develop following the initial move. We can begin with a simple "Zigzag", anticipating the bottom of the "Zigzag" in accordance with tenets learned, then discover the "Zigzag" has become a double "Zigzag". We may find that rallying action develops after three waves of an anticipated "Zigzag" occur. We would then anticipate the development of a "Flat" only to find that a "Triangle" is in the course of development. In essence, it is difficult to determine exactly what type of corrective action will occur until such time as the corrective action is nearly over.

ENLARGEMENT OF CORRECTIONS

It will prove helpful to keep hourly, daily and weekly range charts of the Dow Jones Industrial Average so that one may determine the precise number of waves in the first movement, i.e. either three or five, so we know whether we should anticipate a 5-3-5 count which is likely to produce a "Zigzag", or a 3-3-5 count likely to produce either a "Flat" or an "Irregular Correction".

In Figure 47 we see an "Inverted Flat" with an elongated "C" wave, quite a normal occurrence in the case of the "Flat". The chart on the left-hand side gives the hourly range while the chart on the right only shows the daily range. It can be seen how the hourly range chart discloses many aspects of the movement that cannot be seen in the less sensitive chart.

FIGURE 47

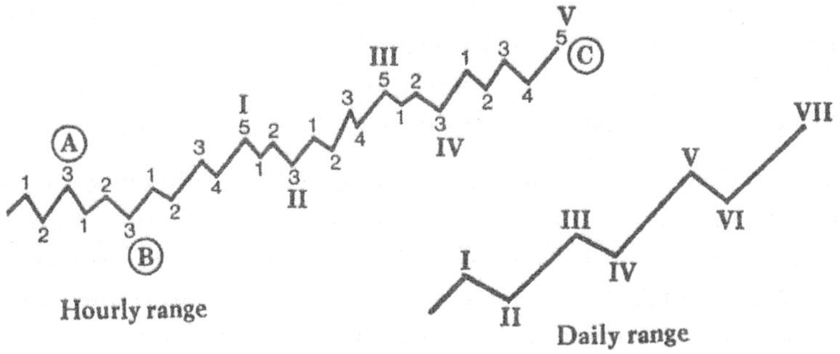

Hourly range

Daily range

Note how, in the daily range chart, the precise composition of the first wave up is not disclosed and the student might erroneously assume that it was composed of five waves of an hourly movement. The daily range of an "inverted flat" would appear as being composed of seven waves, likely to be incorrectly identified. When broken down it can be seen that the entire move is one complete correction, i.e. "A" = three waves, "B" = three waves, "C" = five waves.

Similar behaviour may occur in "Zigzags". A "Zigzag" does not elongate but it may enlarge or double, so to speak. Figure 48 shows how a "Zigzag" may appear over the hourly range when doubled. The same pattern on the daily range would appear incomplete, having three waves down, three waves up, and three waves down. In this instance, the analyst might be on the lookout for a "Triangle" when the more sensitive pattern reveals a completed "Inverted Double Zigzag".

FIGURE 48

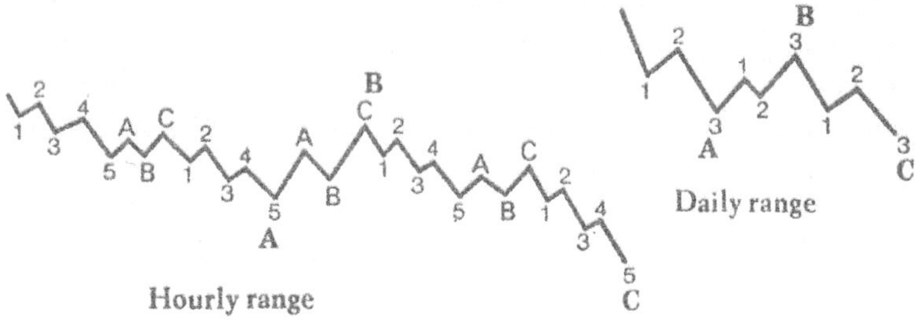

Hourly range

Daily range

It is difficult to determine whether or not a correction is going to become enlarged when it first starts. In fact, at the incipient stages of any type of corrective action, one the most difficult aspects of the Wave Principle is in the precise determination of corrective waves.

The previous rules which have been outlined will help one establish maximum and minimum objectives. In a large majority of cases, corrective action will be completed somewhere within the boundaries of these minimum and maximum objectives. As we know these minimum and maximum objectives can often offer an extremely wide latitude.

Probably the only way in which one can anticipate the precise nature and extent of a corrective move is by relating the incipient stages of the move to its minimum and maximum objective. For example, if a five wave downward move falls significantly short of the peak of impulse Wave 1 of the five waves which the corrective wave is acting against, one would then be on the alert that such a five-wave downward move could develop into a "Double Zigzag".

USE OF THE TIME FACTOR

One can also use the time factor. If a "Zigzag" appears to have been completed in less than the normally expected time period, i.e. 61.8 per cent of the time taken for the primary wave pattern which is being corrected, there is a strong likelihood that such an "A", "B", "C" "Zigzag" is merely the "A" wave of what will subsequently become a "Flat", "Irregular Correction", "Double Three", "Triple Three" or "Triangle".

The time factor should be given a great deal of precedence when attempting to anticipate terminal endings of corrective waves. One may find the development of a "Double Three" over a time period less than would be expected for normal corrective waves. The analyst would then anticipate the development of a "Triple Three". This erratic behaviour of corrective patterns means that it is mandatory to keep sensitive charts on an hourly basis, plotting each move of the Dow Jones Industrial Average in order to dissect each and every wave. But, a word of warning, the minor movements must not cloud your judgement regarding the overriding trend. When becoming involved with the minor movements of these corrective waves, the newcomer to Elliott will experience his most severe difficulty with counting. If ones gets the feeling of "being lost" within the maze of minor movements, step back and consider the position of waves of the higher degree in order to get your bearings once again. Ultimately the "Wave Count" will resolve itself, and, in any case, you will want to use the Wave Principle primarily to take advantage of the big swings in the market. The use of this tool will help you *anticipate* when the big swings are likely to occur.

One final note on the behaviour characteristics of corrective waves should be added at this stage, for it is the point which often confuses a number of Elliott students. A corrective wave need not necessarily take the form of a down swing in a rising market or an up swing in a falling market. The "corrective wave" of a very strong market can often take the form of a sideways movement or even a movement which is trending gently upwards. A correction takes place where there is a strict departure from the momentum of the previous five-wave pattern. Should an "Irregular Correction" develop and this correction is plotted on a daily or weekly chart, the minor components will lose definition and obviously the "Irregular Correction" will appear as an up swing. A "Flat" would give the appearance of merely a sideways movement on an insensitive chart. Gently sloping upward movements, and sideways movements that show a strict departure from the movement of the previous trend and occur at the completion of a five-wave movement, or nine-wave movement if the fifth wave is extended, follow the same behavioural pattern. They have three important waves, and are of the same character – corrective. Figure 49 shows a sideways movement as it might appear on an hourly chart and on a daily range chart.

FIGURE 49

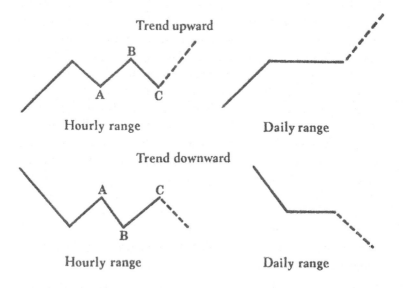

ACTION AFTER THE CORRECTIVE WAVE

When a corrective wave finally runs its course, in most instances terminated by a five-wave downward "C" wave (i.e. when correcting an up trend, but inverted when correcting a down trend), the analyst has many clues as to subsequent action. As I have outlined, a corrective wave that takes the form of a "Triangle" will subsequently produce a very strong "thrust". In application, one could then afford to take more than normal risks when considering exposure to equities when a "Triangle" has just been completed. The same holds true of a sideways movement of "Double Threes" or "Triple Threes".

A "Zigzag" is the type of corrective action that will be witnessed most frequently. When a "Zigzag" occurs as a corrective wave, ordinary strength is expected to follow, the momentum of the movement slower than Wave 1 if the "Zigzag" occurs in Wave 2, and about equal to Wave 1 if the "Zigzag" occurs in Wave 4.

A "Flat" will always produce a stronger than usual subsequent movement, giving the next impulse wave of the Bull Market or Bear Market added strength or weakness respectively, whichever the case may be. Should the "Flat" take place as a "2" wave, the impulse Wave 3 to follow will be as strong, if not stronger, than the first wave of the movement. If the "Flat" takes place in Wave 4, the fifth wave of the movement will be decidedly stronger than either of the other two impulse waves, and likely to develop an extension if no extension had previously occurred in either Wave 1 or Wave 3.

The strongest of all the simpler corrections, indicating subsequent power, is the "Irregular Correction". Any move which follows an "Irregular Correction" should prove to be exceptionally strong and reliable, with corrective action in the sub-waves very weak, while impulse waves of the sub-wave category are likely to be exceptionally strong and protracted in time and amplitude. Additional strength can be anticipated when the "C" wave of an "Irregular Correction" terminates above the level of the "A" wave.

The inherent flexibility of the Wave Principle which allows for further development of corrective waves and impulse waves beyond definable norms, permits the inclusion of various fundamental developments which may happen, yet there is no disruption of the primary pattern of movement. We may see corrective Wave 2 develop in a normal manner, then suddenly a news development causes a rally. The Wave Principle will automatically adjust itself for the rally and change its character in accordance with the input of new fundamental data. A "Zigzag" thus becomes a "Flat", for data has been introduced to strengthen the trend. We then adjust our forecast for what the probable minimum and maximum levels of the "Flat" are likely to be, but the wave remains corrective.

We may be nearing the forecast terminal ending of a five-wave downward move. Without warning an upheaval occurs by Government action or some other development and our "fifth wave" of a "C" wave becomes extended. We then readjust our forecasts in order to anticipate the "double retracement" and "irregular correction" likely to follow the extension. The main trend remains unaltered.

Elliott, in the development of his Wave Principle, despite its complexity, left no stone unturned. Analysts who have used the Wave Principle have commented, "Elliott begins where most other technical methods end." I feel these comments are well justified, if only on his pragmatic approach to the movement of capital markets, a subject which very few analysts understand. To understand the movement of capital markets one must first accept the limitations of available forecasting techniques and devise a method of working within these limitations, avoiding inflexible judgements and the search for an "absolute" at all costs. Elliott understood this principle to a far greater extent than any other analyst of his era. Such an understanding is fundamental to efficient security analysis, and is also fundamental to the effective use of the Wave Principle.

The mechanically-minded chart analyst who seeks absolute rules and methods upon which to make predictions, relying on the repetition of preconceived patterns (which the academics claim are random in their results) will no doubt find the Wave Principle unsatisfactory. Elliott has added so many rules and variations to his basic principle that those who give up in desperation will probably claim the principle has been obliterated by its variations. This attitude would indeed be foolish, for it is in these exceptions and variations that the pragmatic beauty of the Wave Principle actually lies. Elliott has created a working hypothesis for the stock market which can be used to anticipate future share price movements, while being self-adjusting for any events that may occur currently or in the future, in effect, taking into account any possible type of fundamental development that could occur.

Eleven:
The Finishing Touches

"The fact that the future must remain unknown in spite of all efforts does not eliminate the necessity of making an effort. If one is to cope with the future one must attempt to peer into it, however imperfect the vision."

Arnold Bernhard

U NDER THE WAVE Principle, given any distinct set of waves of a recognisable degree, one uses the various tenets and classification methods in order to forecast the periodicity and amplitude of the next wave or series of waves. As the stream of data pours into share prices the wave patterns unfold, with each successive wave, extension or delineation, working its way into the "real world" of share price movements, and each completed wave having a subsequent effect on the waves that will follow. In broad terms, this was Elliott's basic philosophy as applied to the movements of capital markets. It is this philosophy that sets the Wave Principle apart from all other technical approaches to the stock market. In this author's view, Elliott's approach is the only one which can offer the analyst a method of coping with the changing patterns and degrees of uncertainty, which are the unalterable characteristics of the behaviour of capital markets. As one analyst put it, "The only guarantee any investor will ever have is that prices will fluctuate".

Despite the many variations in the Wave Principle, Elliott contended that behind all of this was basic form and continuity. Once an understanding of the basic form was achieved, one could then deal with the deviations from the norm. Elliott found the basic form in the

Fibonacci Summation Series as it related to mass market behaviour patterns and the psychological forces which motivate investors on a broad scale. Cause and effect were part of this basic form. Each wave will enter into the chain of causes which will make the stock market what it is at any given time. The stock market is never right or wrong, it should never be expected to do such and such a thing regardless of subsequent events. Like the Delphic Oracle... the stock market just... *is*. Students of modern capital market theory who insist that relative values do not exist, that there is no such thing as a market that is under valued or over valued, that historical repetitions of price patterns are useless, would certainly agree. The most recent developments in modern capital market theory which now suggest the market may not be random after all – but stochastic – would certainly be compatible with the work of Elliott which seems to transcend all forms of analytical criteria, both technical and fundamental.

Most certainly, distinguishing between waves can often become a "mind-wrenching" complex undertaking leading to analytical desperation, desolation, or both. It will often be the case that the user of the Wave Principle will have to re-adjust his "count" by hindsight in order to make the wave patterns fit the real world of stock market activity as it subsequently unfolds. This has led to the criticism by those who are inexperienced in the use of the Wave Principle that it is of no value, since it can be twisted to fit practically any situation that could possibly exist, in view of what may appear as an unending series of modifications and exceptions to the basic "rules". While there may be something in this criticism – and it would naturally account for the fact that different analysts will come up with different interpretations of the wave breakdowns – is the same criticism not true of *all* forms of stock market analysis?

From time to time the investment community will be greeted with a new method, idea, system, or technique which supposedly will offer the answer to the insoluble problem of consistent profits in the stock market or other capital markets. Many investors will adopt the techniques with unquestioning belief. In days gone by, the P/E Ratio was thought to offer such a panacea, then "discounted cash flow", then "multiple regression analysis", then "cycles", the "Hatch System", the "computer model", the "Coppock System", the "random-walkers", the

"Buy Low-Sell High" method, the "Buy High-Sell Higher" method, the "Buy and Hold" method, the "High Yield" method, the "Hedge" strategy, the "Beta factor", the "Relative strength factor", etc., etc., *ad infinitum, ad nauseam.*

On each occasion investors in large numbers accepted these methods as offering passage to their personal Golconda, only to find bitter disappointment at the end of the journey. So each method in turn was discarded and new ones sought... and the new ones appeared... but the results were always the same. Why? Not because the tools were without purpose. Many of the aforementioned methods were developed by some of the most successful practising analysts in the securities industry. The problem is a lack of understanding of capital markets by the user and an unwillingness to accept the limitations of the tools available in a desire to find the "total" approach to sure and certain profits. As long as capital markets exist, such an approach will *never* exist. It would be wise for the investor to learn this at an early stage. In this author's view Elliott comes closest to achieving such an approach within his maze of variations. For despite the complexities that have been outlined, Elliott did produce some common sense rules for helping the investor establish his bearings if he becomes confused in the "maze".

BREAKDOWN OF THE IMPULSE WAVES

In fact, the entire array of corrective waves and subsequent impulse movements will be found to approximate to a variation of one of the eight impulse wave characteristics shown in Figure 50. We can thus narrow the entire affair down to one out of four possibilities in an up trend, and one of four possibilities in a down trend. So we now find ourselves going from the simplistic to the complex and back to the simplistic again.

FIGURE 50

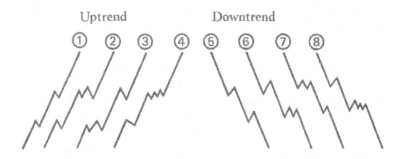

The breakdown of the impulse waves can be categorised as follows:

Up Trend

1. Normal five Wave pattern. Waves 2 and 4 involve the corrective "Zigzag".

2. Normal five Wave pattern. Wave 2 is a "Zigzag", Wave 4 is an "Irregular Correction".

3. Normal five Wave pattern. Wave 2 is a "Flat", Wave 4 is a "Zigzag".

4. Normal five Wave pattern. Wave 2 is a "Zigzag", Wave 4 is a "Triangle".

Down Trend

5. Normal five Wave pattern, Waves 2 and 4 are "Inverted Zigzags".

6. Normal five Wave pattern. Wave 2 is an "Inverted Zigzag", Wave 4 is an "Irregular Correction".

7. Normal five Wave pattern. Wave 2 is an "Inverted Flat", Wave 4 is an "Inverted Zigzag".

8. Normal five Wave pattern. Wave 2 is an "Inverted Zigzag", Wave 4 is a "Triangle".

The only major deviation from the above would occur in the event of one of the impulse waves becoming extended.

By observation one will find the pattern of corrective waves actually alternating, this tendency of "alternation" being a further refinement of the Wave Principle, designed to offer a guide to wave categorisation, and as an aid toward anticipating the likely behaviour of subsequent corrective wave formations.

ELLIOTT'S THEORY OF ALTERNATION

Elliott's theory of alternation has a number of basic applications, the most obvious being the manner in which five-wave formations alternate with three-wave formations as a normative behaviour pattern. According to Elliott, "alternation is a Law of Nature". Leaves on branches of trees appear first on one side of the main stem and then on the opposite side, alternating their position. There is an endless list of examples offered by nature which fortify the principle of alternation but the object of this exercise is the pattern of alternation in human activity.

Bull and Bear Markets alternate. A Bull Market is composed of five waves and a Bear Market of three waves. Thus five and three alternate, this same rule governing all the degrees of the cycle from the tiniest to the largest.

Within the five-wave upward trend, Waves 1, 3 and 5 are upward, Waves 2 and 4 are downward or sideways. Thus the odd numbers alternate with the even numbers.

The above will appear quite obvious. What may not be so obvious is Elliott's concept of alternation as applied to the movement of corrective waves as set down in *Nature's Law*, viz:

> "Waves 2 and 4 are corrective. These two waves alternate in pattern. If Wave 2 is a 'simple' wave, Wave 4 will be complex, or vice versa. A 'simple correction' in the smaller degree is often composed of merely one down swing. If the 2-wave gives this appearance, the 4-wave will involve at least three waves downward or sideways."

In the larger degree, such as complete Bull and Bear Markets of a cycle degree, the corrective waves will naturally be correspondingly larger.

Preparation for the final down swing will often be an extremely tedious affair. Initially one will find a downward movement emanating from the completed five-wave Bull Market. This will comprise the first wave of the "A" wave which will normally be anticipated as a subsequent "A", "B", "C" correction. When broken down, if this "A" wave turns out to be a "Zigzag", then the "B" wave will turn out to be a "Flat" inverted. If Wave "A" is a "Flat", Wave "B" is likely to be an inverted "Zigzag". In any event, regardless of the structure of Waves "A" and "B", Wave "C" will comprise five waves.

Thus in the same manner as Waves 2 and 4 alternate, Waves "A" and "B" in corrective waves of larger formations also alternate. Waves 2 and 4 will take turns in complexity as will Waves "A" and "B".

"Irregular tops" i.e. "irregular corrections" also alternate. As explained in Chapter Nine, an "irregular correction" takes place when the "B" Wave reaches a higher level than the previous peak of the five-wave pattern. Major Bull Market peaks alternate between "orthodox tops" and "irregular tops". Elliott cites the peak of the 1916 Bull Market in the U.S. as having an "irregular top". In 1919 the top was "regular". In 1929 the top was "irregular". In 1937 the top was "regular" again. Each time the Dow-Jones Industrial Averages rose to a new peak, the type of peak alternated with the previous peak. In London, the top of the 1969 Bull Market was "irregular". One can thus expect the top of the next Bull Market to be "regular". In 1969, the F.T.30 reached a level of 520. In May of 1972 that level was reached again by a "B" wave rising to F.T.30 545. Investors were thus given a second chance to get out before the holocaust which took the F.T.30 down in one vicious "C" wave to 146. Since the next top of the F.T.30 is likely to be "regular", there will be no second chance to get out.

Alternation is also expected to take place in the length of waves, and in particular, the extent of corrective action. Logically, corrective Wave 2 should be shorter in time and/or amplitude than corrective Wave 4. If we refer to the January 1975-June 1976 Bull Market movement which produced four waves, this phenomenon is clearly demonstrable. Corrective Wave 2 lasted approximately nine weeks between June and August of 1975 resulting in a "Zigzag" which took 28 per cent from the value of the F.T.30 between the June peak and the August trough.

The pattern was a perfect "Zigzag" having five down waves, 3 up waves, and five down waves.

One would have thus anticipated a much more complex 4 wave, probably extended in direction but shallower in amplitude. What occurred was a "mixed complex triple three" with an elongated "C" wave – in the broad category – a "Flat". It ran the full extent of the maximum expectancy for the 4 wave, terminating at precisely 61.8 per cent of the duration of the preceding 3 Wave. It encompassed its full amplitudinal dimensions, terminating at the top of Wave 1 of the move. However, the amplitude was only 15 per cent as compared with 28 per cent in the case of the 2 wave. Elliott's theory of alternation developed with clockwork precision in that particular instance… and many others.

Elliott's theory of alternation goes a long way in helping one anticipate the likely formation of subsequent corrective waves, this being the most elusive aspect of the Wave Principle. Given a simple corrective 2 wave we are then on the alert for a troublesome 4 wave. Given a 2 wave which falls short of the maximum time span we are then placed on the alert that the 4 wave is likely to run its full time span.

Should an irregular correction develop in a 2 wave, the 4 wave will have a normal top. Bull Market peaks and Bear Market troughs will thus alternate in the development of orthodox or irregular tops and bottoms.

Translating this into practical application on the London Stock Exchange in June 1976, the approaching intermediate top should be a simple "Zigzag", while the Bear Market bottom which will succeed it should turn out to be an inverted irregular correction.

A. Hamilton Bolton adds a most succinct touch to Elliott's theory of alternation: "The writer is NOT convinced that alternation is INEVITABLE in types of waves in larger formations, but there are frequent enough cases of alternation to suggest that one should look for it rather than the contrary."

I would like to add that the *lack of inevitability* in most of Elliott's tenets provides the Wave Principle with the type of flexibility which is mandatory for dealing with capital market movements. Seeking absolute inevitability in any form of analytical principle is bound to lead to totally unsatisfactory results. As the casino operator asked the gambler who insisted he had found a system for beating the roulette wheel, "Your system may be great, but can you teach it to the roulette wheel?"

When the analyst of stock market trends learns to substitute the phrase "probability of occurrence" for the words "predict" and "forecast", a giant step will have been taken in the field of trend analysis.

ERRONEOUS COUNTING

A particular "grey" area of Elliott's work appears in the time relationship between corrective waves and the preceding "impulse waves". Normally, one would expect a corrective wave to be shorter in time than the preceding impulse wave. In most of Elliott's examples of normative behaviour, both in *Nature's Law* and *The Wave Principle*, the time frame and the amplitudinal frame would appear to confirm this view. However, when Elliott goes on to apply his principles to actual stock market action, there are several examples where the time frame of the "corrective waves" seems to encompass periods which extend beyond the normal relationship to the period of the preceding impulse wave. This tendency is most notable when an irregular correction develops.

In *Nature's Law* Elliott sets down the hypothesis:

> "The three impulse waves, 1, 3 and 5 are seldom of the same length. One of the three is usually considerably longer than either of the other two. It is important to note that Wave 3 is never shorter than both Wave 1 and Wave 5. For example, when Wave 3 is shorter than either Wave 1 or Wave 5, as in the graph below (Figure 51), the correct method of counting is as follows:"

FIGURE 51

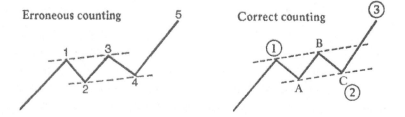

While Elliott states that Wave 3 can never be shorter than both Waves 1 and 5, he goes on to say that if Wave 3 *appears* to be shorter than *either* Wave 1 or 5, it is necessary to re-classify the count. The under-developed 3 wave actually extends the corrective 2 wave. Whereas it may have originally appeared that Wave 2 was a complete correction in itself, the 3 wave which is shorter than both Wave 1 and Wave 5 is actually the "B" wave of an "irregular correction". What was originally thought to be the "4 wave" becomes the "C" wave. Instead of completing the pattern with a five-wave count, the 5 wave becomes Wave 3. The abbreviated 3 wave actually borrows two waves from the succeeding movement.

In the above illustration, another cardinal violation takes place which confirms that the original count was erroneous. That is, the 4 wave overlaps Wave 1. The fact that a 4 wave should never overlap the peak of Wave 1 is one of the Elliott tenets which supercedes most others. Both in *Nature's Law, The Wave Principle* and the works of others who have used and observed the Wave Principle, no deviations or exceptions are permitted with regard to the rule of the "impulse wave" relationship, i.e. Waves 1 and 5 should be shorter than Wave 3. Wave 3 can at times be shorter than Waves 1 or 5 but never shorter than both. The maximum extent of a 4 wave will be to the peak of the preceding Wave 1. With all of Elliott's exceptions, additions, refinements, etc., these simple basic impulse wave relationships remain constant.

Thus should a 4 wave dip below the peak of the 1 wave, one knows that an error in counting has taken place, and therefore a complete recount is necessary. The same would hold true if we find a pattern of development where Wave 3 is shorter than both the 1 wave and the 5 wave.

The remaining point of obscurity is whether the time frame relationship was involved. It is fairly clear that Elliott was referring to the amplitudinal relationship in accordance with his illustrations. However, it would appear that if a time scale were placed underneath his examples, the fact that the 2 wave borrows two more waves from the succeeding movement would mean that the actual time span of the "irregular correction" extended beyond the duration of the development of Wave 1. In this respect the "corrective wave" is actually shorter in amplitude but longer in time than the wave it is correcting.

If one refers to Elliott's classification of the Super Cycle in the U.S. from 1857 to 1928 in Part IV of the Appendix it becomes clear than in the Wave Principle, amplitude of the waves takes precedence over time:

SUPER CYCLE CLASSIFICATION, 1857-1964

Cycle Wave I 1857-1864 (7 years)
Cycle Wave II 1864-1877 (13 years)
Cycle Wave III 1877-1881 (4 years)
Cycle Wave IV 1881-1896 (15 years)
Cycle Wave V 1896-1928 (32 years)

In Elliott's own analysis of this Super Cycle Wave it can be seen quite clearly that both corrective waves exceeded the preceding impulse waves by vast time spans, and Wave III is shorter in time than both Waves I and V. However, Wave III was smaller in amplitude than Wave V, but greater in amplitude than Wave I, on the logarithmic scale. Obviously considerable latitude is allowable for time frame relationships between corrective waves and the impulse waves they are correcting. There is no allowable deviation from amplitudinal relationships.

This point is extremely important, for the most serious errors in counting are likely to occur when dealing with irregular corrections. Unless one pays strict attention to the amplitude of the 3 wave, the "B" wave of an "irregular correction" could be interpreted as the 3 wave. The actual 3 wave would become a 5 wave. We would be anticipating a full "A", "B", "C" Bear Market, if an "irregular correction" was counted incorrectly. All we would normally expect would be the subsequent development of Wave 4 and Wave 5 when counting correctly.

"FAILURES"

"Failures" are not what they sound like. When a "failure" occurs this does not mean an error has arisen in the method or that a mistake has been made. A "failure" occurs when an impulse wave weakens and falls short of its normal objective.

In Figure 52 it would appear that the fifth wave has failed to develop and a Bull Market took place encompassing three upward waves followed by five waves downward. There are two things wrong with that interpretation. Firstly, a Bull Market would never be composed of three waves, always five; and secondly, a corrective Bear Market wave would comprise three waves rather than five. What has actually occurred has been a "failure" in the fifth wave, the subsequent decline stealing two waves from the advance. The correct count is shown on the diagram underneath. A breakdown of the pattern to the next lower degree will help you resolve the problem of whether the "B" wave was a 5 wave or not.

FIGURE 52

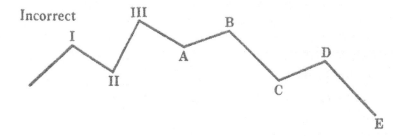

Elliott's discussion of "failures" was limited to only a small mention in the 1938 edition of *The Wave Principle*. In *Nature's Law* published in 1946, no mention at all was made of this phenomenon. A. J. Frost, in the 1967 *Supplement to the Bank Credit Analyst*, does take the matter of "failures" a bit further.

Although Elliott's claim was that "failures" are rare, Frost states "failures are not uncommon" and give warning to the analyst of impending strength or weakness, depending on whether the "failure" occurs in a Bull or Bear cycle. According to Frost, a "failure" occurs when the fifth wave in a Bull cycle fails to penetrate the top of the third wave in the cycle. In a "Bear cycle", the "failure" occurs when the fifth wave of the "C" wave fails to penetrate the low of the 3 wave in the "C" wave.

While Elliott never elaborated on the point, the empirical evidence would suggest that "failures" are limited to fifth wave developments, and only occur if the fifth wave fails to penetrate the peak of the third wave which preceded.

"Failures" have often been ignored by students of the Wave Principle. This was probably due to Elliott's brief coverage of the matter and its complete omission from *Nature's Law*. A. Hamilton Bolton, writing extensively on the Wave Principle for over 15 years, also neglected the aspect of "failures". Nevertheless, recognition of the "failure" is vital, for the Wave Principle can become a "hodge-podge" unless one is constantly on the look-out for the possibility of a "failure" developing in the fifth wave of a movement. In the same manner as "erroneous counting" can drastically change the possibilities of future wave progressions, so too can the non-recognition of a "failure". Left undetected, a fifth wave "failure" will produce the effect of rendering a five-wave count as a three-wave count. This would mean the 4 wave of the corrective wave looks like the 2 wave of the next higher degree. This further example of erroneous counting would compound itself until the count becomes baffling and totally undecipherable. In view of its readily recognisable appearance, the "failure" should rank as one of the more important tenets of Elliott's Wave Principle.

"THRUSTS"

"Thrusts" were noted as occurring predominantly after the completion of a "Triangle" or "Horizontal" movement. All during the movement, a contraction in volume takes place reflecting investor indecision and reluctance. Suddenly, some investors tip the balance, and all others follow the lead in a powerful move which is called a "Thrust". In essence, a "Thrust" is a dynamic move which follows a period of hesitation or consolidation, which in technical terms is likely to be one of accumulation preceding the "mark-up" phase. The very nature of a "Thrust" is one of greater than ordinary power, therefore corrections within the "Thrust" are likely to be of sub-normal duration and amplitude. Since a "Thrust" follows corrective action it is obvious that "Thrusts" only occur as impulse waves, primarily impulse Wave 5 since the "Triangle" or "Horizontal" is most likely to be a 4 wave.

"Thrusts" can also occur following an "irregular correction" where the "C" wave produces an upward "Zigzag". A "Thrust" can also follow a "Flat". Elliott claimed a "Thrust" would follow naturally from a "Triangle" and that "Triangles" and "Flats" had similar technical implications with regard to the subsequent strength of succeeding impulse waves. The reasoning is fairly clear. Both of the aforementioned patterns are likely to be of sub-normal amplitude, indicative of a market which is gathering strength. Should corrective action only be shallow in either the 2 wave or 4 wave encompassing only sub-normal corrective action, it stands to reason that a warning of strong ensuing action is being flashed. Corrective action will take the form of a normal "Zigzag" at least 50 per cent of the time within the context or the varying cycle degrees. The rest of the corrective action will show a variety of "Flats", "Triangles", "Horizontals", "Irregular Corrections" and upward "Zigzags". In the case of the "Irregular Correction" and the upward "Zigzag" the signal that a "Thrust" is likely to follow will be an abbreviated "C" wave. The "C" wave will end above the trough of the "A" wave (assuming an upward impulse set of waves), and the bigger the gap the greater the power of the ensuing "Thrust". All bets would be off for the "Thrust" if the "C" wave fell below the trough of the "A" wave in either case.

VOLUME

Elliott's treatment of volume was relatively sparse, his main concern being the use of volume in order to quantify the wave count and to provide clues for the further possible development of existing trends.

Volume was mentioned in the discussion of corrective waves, particularly "Triangles" and "Horizontal" movements. It is the normal tendency for volume to diminish during the transition of a corrective phase. Generally, when the volume of trading reaches an historically low level within the corrective phase one can conclude that such a corrective phase is nearing completion.

The tendency for volume to diminish during a corrective phase can often help in the identification of extended waves before they become fully extended. An extended fifth wave will take on four additional waves producing a count of nine (see Chapter Eight). When the seventh wave is completed, a counting error can often occur since it will be difficult to determine with precision whether or not the two additional waves to the five-wave count are actually two waves of an extension, or the "A" and "B" wave of an "Irregular Correction". Figure 53 shows the two possible interpretations of the same pattern.

FIGURE 53

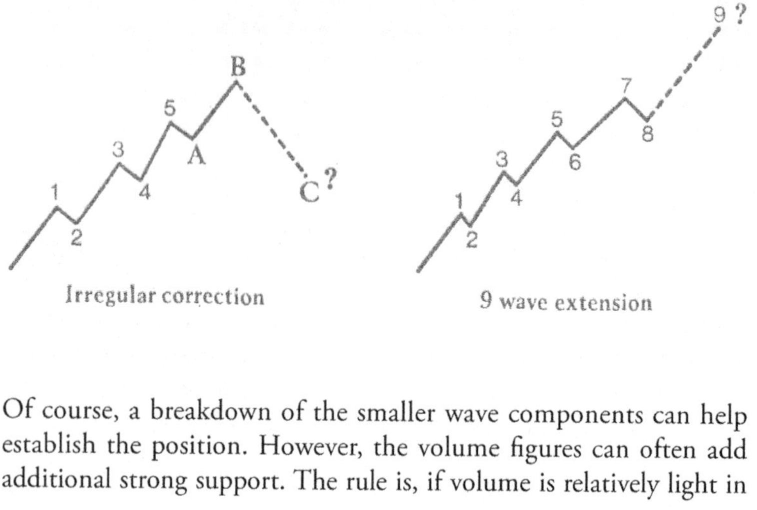

Irregular correction   9 wave extension

Of course, a breakdown of the smaller wave components can help establish the position. However, the volume figures can often add additional strong support. The rule is, if volume is relatively light in the seventh wave then it is more than likely that an "Irregular Correction" is taking place and the next move will be the downward "C" wave, with a possibility of extending to the peak of Wave 1, for the "Irregular Correction" will be taking place as a 4 wave. On the other hand if volume has expanded on Wave 7, an extension is generating. One would then anticipate a down wave with a maximum risk level to the peak of Wave 5, followed by another up swing which would produce a new high in the move. On this occasion, volume figures will offer a very valuable guide. Elliott adds, however, "…when markets are abnormally 'thin', the usual volume signals are sometimes deceptive".

According to Elliott, characteristics of volume are very impressive when considered in conjunction with the five-wave cycle. For example, during an advance or decline of an important magnitude, volume will tend to increase during the first wave, decrease during the second wave, expand during the third wave, contract again during the fourth wave and expand once more in the fifth and final wave. When the fifth and final wave is reached, volume is likely to continue rising; however, the price action will suddenly become lethargic. We are then warned that an important reversal is in the making.

In general, price and volume must agree. While the progression in volume is one of expansion during the up waves and contraction during down waves, one should take serious note of the volume relationships of the impulse waves and the corrective waves. While Wave 2 should contract significantly below the volume recorded during Wave 1, the volume of Wave 4 should be less than Wave 3 but greater than Wave 2. The volume figure for Wave 3 should be the highest of the cycle, significantly greater than that of Wave 1 but only marginally different from Wave 5. When the fifth wave of an advance is completed it is unlikely that the volume of the fifth wave will exceed the volume of the third wave by any significant amount. On many occasions the volume of the fifth wave will be less than that of the third wave.

So long as volume continues to expand one can assume a further advance in the price action is likely. When the price action advances but volume does not, the move is nearing a terminal phase.

Elliott's concept of normal volume behaviour throughout a five wave cycle can be seen in Figure 54. Note the manner in which volume should continue to advance during Waves 1 and 3 but become laboured at relatively high volume levels for the entirety of the fifth wave. Also note that, although volume should contract during the fourth wave of the pattern, even at the terminal point of Wave 4, volume remains high.

FIGURE 54

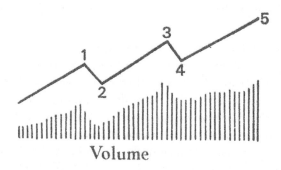

Volume

During a Bear Market, volume tendencies can be expected to be just the opposite of those which govern Bull Market behaviour. As the corrective wave (usually defined as a "Bear Market") progresses, volume will shrink to lower and lower levels. During the early stages of the Bear move, one will find volume expanding on the downward impulse waves and contracting on the corrective upwaves. However as the Bear Market draws to a close, there will be a shift in the volume characteristics. During the "C" wave of a Bear Market, the volume of trading is likely to be far less than that of the preceding "A" wave and less than the "B" wave. It is a popular fallacy that Bear Markets end in one shattering selling climax. This is not really so. The fallacy probably developed out of the normally vicious "C" wave, a characteristic of most Bear Market movements. The "C" wave of the Wall Street crash was probably the most devastating on record. The "C" wave that took place in London between 1972 and 1975, bringing to an end the cycle Bear Market which began in 1969, was another disastrous move. To suggest that a "selling climax" was in the course of development for three years would not be particularly helpful. The bottom of the "C" wave in both of these cases did not end in an earth shattering dumping of shares... that happened much earlier. At the bottom of the market in 1932 and 1974, the Bear Market ended in a whisper when the last private investor who intended to sell sold the last share he had to sell.

William C. Garrett, author of *Investing for Profit with Torque Analysis of Stock Market Cycles* bases much of cyclical work around the Elliott Wave hypothesis but claims Elliott's treatment of volume is the one major weakness. According to Garrett, the key to accurate wave classification lies in the volume figures. Garrett weaves the subject of volume into extravagant complexity, dealing with the economic influences, seasonal influences, cyclical volume patterns and other factors. In the final analysis it is debatable whether or not Garrett's observations have added much to the very simple treatment of volume provided by Elliott.

MOVING AVERAGES

A valuable contribution to wave classification which was neither a part of Elliott's work or that of A. Hamilton Bolton's is suggested by A. J. Frost, this being the incorporation of moving averages. Frost uses the 55-hour moving average and the 89-hour moving average, the purpose of which is to smooth out the erratic minor waves in order to determine the more important overriding trends.

Although called a 55-hour Moving Average, this being a Fibonacci number, in actuality Frost was dealing with a 10-Day Moving Average of Closing prices on the Dow-Jones Industrial Averages which he claims was for all practical purposes equivalent to 55 hours.

When applying the concept to the London Stock Exchange the same would not hold true, since there are seven hourly quotes during an eight-hour trading session. Thus the 10-day moving average would be the equivalent of 80 trading hours rather than 55 as in the U.S.

Even so I would still advocate the use of the 10-day moving average for cross-verification of the wave counts in London. Although the hourly moves do not represent one of the number "5" numbers in the Fibonacci Summation Series, nor does the 10-day total, the value lies in smoothing out the minor movements that occur within the confines of a short term trading period of, say, two to three weeks which by themselves move in segments that are not always clear. A great deal can be gained by using the crossing of the average as representative of the pivotal points of each wave. In this way one can avoid being mesmerised by the sub-minor fluctuations that occur within intermediate wave junctures.

It should be a general rule that one should never "force" a Wave Count. Never try to fit a pattern into what would be desirable under ideal Elliott conditions unless the pattern is fairly definable. The incorporation of this mechanical moving average will assist in making the waves more definable, so providing a good starting point for more detailed analysis.

As you progress with the use of the Wave Principle, there will be many occasions when the "count" appears so arbitrary that the number of permutations are practically useless if one attempts to adopt a strategy to the fit the wave structure. There are many reasons why this can happen. One should expect it to happen. By the same token, one should not dismiss the Wave Principle as a result. At times the message of the stock market will unfold with astonishing clarity. At other times the market's message will be vague and obscure. This will be reflected in the wave structure of the market. One must not expect the market to "tip its hand" every hour of every day of the week. Attempting to seek an answer for all price action when no answer is available, subsequently trying to forecast the unforecastable is one of the most serious errors an investor can make. When the wave structure is not clear and the count not discernable, step back, look at the longer term structure… if necessary, discard the study of share price movement for a time, awaiting those periods of readily definable trend action which will provide you with an optimal opportunity. The use of the 10-day moving average will help in this respect. With the Wave Principle, we are not trying to "beat the market", we are trying to *join it*! Opportunities will be offered by share price movements in accordance with the action of the market place… not necessarily in accordance with the terms we would like to impose. Recognise this aspect of stock market behaviour… wait for the market to provide you with the opportunities you may be seeking… don't expect the market to provide those opportunities just because it is *your* decision to suddenly invest when "things look bullish", or you've suddenly come into some money, or it is the end of a week, or the beginning of a new tax year, etc. Let the action of the market tell *you* when to make a commitment… don't expect the stock market to behave in a manner which is suited to your convenience. Bear in mind two truisms of share price behaviour:

1. "The market will always do what it has to do to make the majority wrong."

2. "The market spends 90 per cent of the time making up its mind where to go and 10 per cent of the time going there".

These two bits of stock market dogma might help you gain a better perspective of share price movements.

Over the shorter term, the 10-day moving average of Closing prices will help you sort the wheat from the chaff in the wave structure. Over the intermediate term an 89-day moving average is recommended. The 89-day moving average, used in conjunction with the 10-day moving average should help you to delineate both sub-minor and minor movements of an erratic nature. Whenever the 10-day moving average crosses the 89-day moving average it is a strong indication that a possible change in the market's trend has developed. According to Frost, such crossing will indicate the beginning of a new wave formation of intermediate or even higher degree.

When dealing with a 2 wave and a 4 wave it is always wise to check and see if the D.J.30 has actually crossed from above to below in order to confirm that corrective action has begun, when the main trend is upward. It is equally wise to cross-check with the moving average in order to confirm that such corrective action is complete. When a 2 wave begins over the intermediate term one should expect to see the D.J.30 dip below the 10-day moving average, following shortly after the beginning of the corrective "A" wave of the "A", "B", "C" 2 wave. The same would hold true for the 4 wave. When the corrective action is complete, the 10-day moving average will serve to confirm such a completion, lagging the development of the new set of five waves.

When using these moving averages as a confirming indicator to the Wave Count one must watch for the following sequence:

1. A corrective down wave will obviously begin upon the completion of five waves.

2. After the corrective down wave has begun, additional credibility will be given to the probable depth of the move when the D.J.30 crosses the 10-day moving average.

3. If the corrective action is one of a larger degree the D.J.30 will not only cross the 10-day moving average but will cross the 89-day moving average.

4. Additional credibility will be given to the extent of an important down swing when the 10-day average crosses the 89-day moving average.

5. A corrective wave will be completed at the 5 wave of a "C" wave.

6. Confirmation of such a completion will be provided when the D.J.30 crosses from below to above the 10-day moving average although the new up trend may well be established by that time.

7. Should the corrective action have been of a large degree it will be likely that the D.J.30 had penetrated the 10-day moving average and the 89-day moving average during the initial stages of the correction. It will therefore be necessary to see the D.J.30 recover to a level above the 89-day moving average and the 10-day moving average in order to confirm the previous corrective action as complete. It must be recognised that the new trend will have been underway for a time before such confirmation is available.

8. In the case of a corrective wave of a large degree, final confirmation that the correction is complete is made when the 10-day moving average crosses above the 89-day moving average.

9. To confirm the durability of an intermediate up trend, the 10-day moving average and the 89-day moving average must remain "in-phase", the shorter term average travelling in an upward trend above the longer term average. When the opposite occurs a down trend is in effect.

In the words of A. J. Frost, "Corrective Patterns are often complex, and patience pays."

ANCILLARY INDICATORS

The Wave Principle is the only tool which this author is aware of which is actually capable of forecasting *future* price movements. Practically every other analytical tool is merely a *measure* of current market strength or weakness which technicians have adopted, claiming a tendency for future predictions based on a simple hypothesis, to wit, "A trend in motion will stay in motion... until it changes."

To my mind, this latter approach is totally unsatisfactory unless one can devise a method enabling one to *anticipate* the all important... "change". Don't be fooled by the claims of technicians in this respect.

The Wave Principle has been designed for the sole purpose of anticipating *future* trend changes both in time and amplitude, based on a hypothesis that goes far beyond the aforementioned. In this respect, the use of the Wave Principle with respect to ancillary technical market conditions can be extremely helpful, particularly if such indicators have lead qualities.

The use of the Wave Principle on any of the following supplementary technical indicators can be of immense value when attempting clarification of the Wave Count in the primary indices:

1. Advance and Decline (Cumulative flow line) Index.

2. Positive Volume Index.

3. Negative Volume Index.

4. Accumulation and Distribution Index.

5. Momentum Index.

6. Net New Highs and New Lows (Running Total).

Several indicators have not been included since they would not be applicable to a Wave Count in view of their structure.

Twelve:

Practical Application
of the Wave Principle

"Behaviour of Waves has been fairly well explored but application is in its infancy."

R. N. Elliott

THE GENESIS OF the stock market was a large tree under which buyers and sellers of shares in various different companies would meet in order to transact their business. For a time, the tree was adequate for the purpose, fulfilling the pure function of a market-place where men could go and effect their transactions. But even then we were in a growth-oriented environment, and before long the business of dealing in stocks and shares expanded and the tree was abandoned in favour of a nearby coffee house, in turn necessitating the need for a code of dealing practices.

Somewhere along the line the business of prophecy was added to the business of dealing in stocks and shares. Why a share dealer was expected to know anything more about the future behaviour of the shares in which he dealt than a fish pedlar about the idiosyncrasies of fish, has always been a problem and a curse. Nevertheless, that's what happened and since then the prediction business has almost swamped and ruined the brokerage business.

Most of the work that has been published on the Wave Principle deals with the manner in which one can predict the future by projecting the various waves and their extent. A. Hamilton Bolton, A.J. Frost, Charles

Collins, Russell Hall, E.N. White and Ed Tabell have made voluminous efforts in outlining past wave patterns in an effort to forecast future wave terminations, something of which I too am guilty. Naturally, one can have great fun by keeping an hourly chart on the movement of the Dow Jones Industrial Average, and watching the various wave patterns and their permutations develop. There will certainly be a feeling of reward when one makes a "prediction" and finds the wave has terminated within a tenth of a point of the forecast move, as will happen on many occasions when the Wave Principle has been mastered. The whole affair should prove to be a marvellous mental exercise, as does completing crossword puzzles for those who are that way inclined. Unfortunately, in many instances, individuals will presuppose that this type of forecasting will enable them to make money in the stock market. Unless you are a writer of stock market newsletters, or an analyst for a stock broker touting business by displaying the accuracy of your predictions, you must draw a distinct line between the money making business and the predicting business. There is a large divergence between the two.

At worst the Wave Principle will prove to be a most rewarding tool, by using which one can make future predictions and then sit back and see whether or not these predictions actually materialise. At best, the Wave Principle will enable you to develop a cohesive strategy to incorporate with long-term, intermediate-term and short-term goals which ever is your inclination. You will attempt to detect optimal short-term buying and selling levels. You will be on the alert for intermediate terminal junctures in order to adjust balances in your portfolio.

The long-term investor will only be interested in participating in the market during the major cyclical moves, switching to fixed interest securities or other money market instruments when a move is complete. He will remain in these instruments until such time as the cyclical forces have spent their effects, anticipating a period when he will re-invest for the next long cycle up swing. In this respect, the long-term investor might spend three to five years invested in common stocks and two to four years out of them. It is this latter aspect of the Wave Principle that should be of major concern rather than its predictive value.

TERMINAL ENDINGS

The number five should be indelibly engraved upon your investment thinking. The big five-wave down move will provide you with the optimal buying point. The five-wave up-move, possibly extended by five more waves and five on top of that, will present you with the optimal selling opportunity. No matter what other factors concern your investment decision-making process, economic, fundamental, technical or whatever, you must always be on the look-out for the completion of the all important five-wave move, down or up. If it makes it easier, think of two successive rallies and then one third and final rally. The third rally will be your signal to start selling your shares.

In a Bear Market envisage three successive plunges downward, each interrupted by some brief rallying action. That last down wave will tell you the end of the Bear Market is coming. There is nothing more to think about, nothing more to be concerned with. The empirical evidence in favour of terminal endings occurring in precisely the manner suggested by Elliott is nothing short of overwhelming.

In *The Wave Principle* Elliott creates a hypothetical example for the long-term investor who may have purchased shares in 1921, near the bottom of the Bear Market which had followed the 1918-20 peak inflation in Europe and America.

> "Let us assume that the investor has correctly established a long position in June 1921. From his study of the Grand Super Cycle (as shown in the following chart), he sees that the market started as a Super Cycle movement in 1857 and that Cycle movements one, two three and four of the entire Super Cycle movement have been completed.

FIGURE 55: GRAND SUPER CYCLE OF 5 SUPER CYCLE WAVES

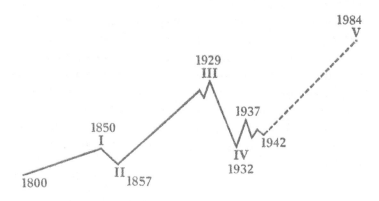

"The fifth Cycle movement started in 1896 and is nearly completed, in that four primary waves have elapsed from 1896 to 1921. Primary movement number five is just commencing. It will be made up of five Intermediate movements. Intermediate movement number five will not only terminate the full Primary movement, but it will also terminate a full Cycle movement and a full Super Cycle. The period ahead, in other words, promises to be quite interesting.

"Based upon his study of Primary movements, one and three preceding, the fifth one now getting under way, the investor has some gauge as to the extent and length of the movement, although, as previously mentioned, these are but rough guides due to modifying events which serve to differentiate one wave of a certain degree from another wave of the same degree. A more certain guide, however, can be derived from channelling. The Super Cycle running from 1957 as seen in the preceding chart of the Axe-Houghton-Burgess Index, has completed four waves of a lesser degree (Cycle movements), and thus by connecting exposed contacts of wave terminals two and four of the Super Cycle and drawing a parallel line across the terminal point of wave three, an upper parallel is established, about which line the fifth cycle, or that running from 1896, should end, thus completing wave five of the Super Cycle movement.

> Similarly, the Cycle movement from 1896 has completed four waves (Primary movements) so that, as for the Super Cycle, it can be given its final upper channel line about which the fifth primary movement now under way should terminate."

R. N. Elliott, The Wave Principle

Well, the period ahead of which Elliott was writing was indeed "interesting". It produced one of the longest, most glorious bull markets in the history of the stock market between 1921-9, resulting in a 400 per cent move in the Dow-Jones Industrial Averages and an extremely long and powerful move in London. It also presaged the "Great Crash" and its devastating after effects along with a similar incident in London. The cyclical continuity of the two markets was practically identical even though the British experience was not as severe as in the U.S.

It is ironic that Elliott should have chosen the period of 1921 for his illustration. During 1921 there was a world recession going on as the aftermath of the peak inflation brought about by the period following World War 1. There was an oil crisis between the U.S. and Mexico and labour problems had reached a nadir. The money supply had run rampant in the post-war years and was followed by a crisis of confidence in the banking system while Governments the world over considered that the greatest threat to society was inflation. So similar to today's experiences was the economic and social environment during the 1930s that *Forbes Magazine* recently reproduced a series of newspaper headlines from that period demonstrating how these same headlines could actually be appearing in today's newspapers.

THE NEXT TEN YEARS

The "Great Crash" of 1929 marked the end of the Super Cycle which began in 1857. In 1932 a new Super Cycle began. As the 1920-2 Bear Market produced Wave 4 of the 1857-1920 Super Cycle, so too has the most recent Bear Market in London produced Wave IV of the Super Cycle which began in 1932. Thus, once again, in the same manner we are embarking on the fifth and final wave of a Super Cycle which will produce a fifth Cycle Wave and a fifth Primary Wave, likely to be composed of five Intermediate Waves. Once again some subtle irony appears, for whichever way we like to construct our cyclical count, either through the Fibonacci Series, by constructing a channel with tangents drawn to the wave terminal of the 1932 cycle, by using the economic wave of Kondratieff, Kitchin or Juglar,... the answer comes out the same... a terminal point in the cycle of 1984.

The cyclicality of the period that lies ahead is likely to be even more "interesting" than the period Elliott was referring to, for not only have we now begun the first Intermediate Wave of the fifth Primary Wave, of the fifth Cycle Wave of the fifth Super Cycle Wave, but this period also acts as the culmination of the fifth Grand Super Cycle Wave. In 1800 the Grand Super Cycle began. By 1928 Britain had completed three waves in the Grand Super Cycle, five waves in the Super Cycle, five waves in the Cycle, and five waves of the Primary. The 1920-2 market decline produced the "A", "B", "C" correction of the Super Cycle move and also Wave IV of the Grand Super Cycle. The Super Cycle which began in 1932 is actually Wave V of the Grand Super Cycle.

Should the forecast be correct, by 1984 we will see the completion of the Grand Super Cycle. This cycle being of 184 years in duration, the corrective action to be anticipated would have to be sufficient to eliminate all the excesses of this period of history, and according to the tenets of Elliott, *would be greater than any corrective action that has taken place during the course of the cycle.*

I certainly have no intention of being fatalistic about the entire affair. At this stage I will merely play the role of ostrich and stick my head in the sand by saying, I am just the student conveying the words of the master. If Elliott's treatment of the Wave Principle in its Grand Super Cycle context proves correct we have two things to look forward to. Firstly, a Bull Market of the dimensions and time span similar to that experienced by the U.S. market preceding the "Great Crash", i.e. about six more years of rapidly rising prices as the level of equities catches up to the previous rate of inflation in the U.K. Secondly, a massive collapse that will make the 1972-5 "C" wave, look like a Teddy Bear's picnic. But first things first. Let us set down some precedents of how one should handle the market in the remaining years of the Bull Phase. We should all know what to do when it terminates. The object at this time is to make sure sales are not made prematurely and the investor gets the maximum return on capital employed from the move that remains. If you are a long term investor all you have to do is stick with it, making sure you are not tempted to liquidate your holdings too soon. So your job will be to spot the terminal point when it comes.

SEQUENCE FOR SELLING

As a guide, bear in mind the following sequence:

1. The Primary movement will be made up of five Intermediate waves. Selling is not to be considered until four Intermediate waves have been witnessed and the fifth wave is underway.

2. When the fourth Intermediate wave has terminated and the fifth gets underway, it will be composed of five lesser degree or Minor waves. Selling should not be considered until the fifth Minor wave is underway.

3. When the fourth Minor wave of the fifth Intermediate wave has terminated, and the fifth Minor wave gets underway, it will not terminate until five Minute waves have been witnessed. Selling is not to be considered ahead of the fifth Minute wave.

4. It is probable that the fifth Minute wave of the fifth Minor wave of the Intermediate will be made up of five Minuette waves, based upon the movement on the hourly chart. The fifth wave of the Minuette movements will be composed of five Sub-Minuette waves. To reach the extreme top of the Cycle Wave which started in January 1975, one waits for completion of the fifth Sub-Minuette Wave, of the fifth Minuette Wave, of the fifth Minute Wave, of the fifth Minor Wave, of the fifth Intermediate Wave of the fifth Primary Wave.

5. The fifth wave of a Grand Super Cycle movement, of a Super Cycle movement, of a Cycle movement of a Primary

movement, will generally penetrate or "throwover" the upper channel line established for the termination limit of the fifth Grand Super Cycle Wave, the fifth Super Cycle Wave and the fifth Cycle Wave. Since the Cycle movement which started in January 1975 will end a Grand Super Cycle movement as well as a Super Cycle movement, it may be anticipated that such Cycle movement will not have ended until it has carried prices (on a logarithmic scale) above the upper channel lines of the Grand Super Cycle and the Super Cycle. Likewise, the fifth Intermediate movement of the Primary movement which began in June 1976, should penetrate or "throwover" the upper channel line established for it, such channel intersection occurring at approximately 454 in the Financial Times Industrial Ordinary Share Index on the October 1976 time span at the time of writing.

6. Terminal points of the fifth wave of a Grand Super Cycle, Super Cycle, Cycle and Primary movements are usually accompanied by heavy trading volume relative to prior waves of each such movement. Intense volume should therefore be witnessed during and near the peak of the fifth Intermediate wave of the Primary movement which is now underway.

7. With these general rules in mind, the investor should now watch the market unfold, plotting its weekly and monthly movement in order to keep abreast of each Intermediate move as it occurs. As we draw closer to the forecast terminal of Intermediate Wave 5, likely to occur during the autumn of 1976, the intermediate term trader should consult the hourly charts with a view to liquidating holdings at the fifth Sub-Minuette wave of the fifth Minuette wave of the fifth Minute wave of the fifth Minor wave of the fifth Intermediate wave. As of July 1976 the Financial Times Industrial Ordinary Share Index had just begun the third Minute wave of the first Minor wave of the fifth Intermediate wave. During the autumn of 1976 we should witness the final completion of the fifth Intermediate Wave, thus presaging a down swing which will correct the excesses accumulated since the beginning of the move in January 1975. The Intermediate term trader would

be wise to liquidate holdings with a view toward repurchasing when the down swing is completed. This down swing is likely to be a simple "Zigzag", since it will represent Wave 2 of the Primary movement. Given that the Primary movement will have encompassed approximately 22 months, the maximum expectancy for leg 3 of the movement would be about 14 months, producing a maximum amplitude to the tip of the fifth leg of the Intermediate term movement which was F.T. 30 368. Therefore, when this Intermediate movement is complete, the correction that follows is not likely to produce an overly severe bear wave, but one which would represent nothing more than an Intermediate term trading opportunity. Long term investors are not advised to consider liquidation merely at the peak of a fifth wave of an Intermediate term movement.

8. While this may appear an exceptionally long-range forecast, longer term investors would not be advised to consider any major liquidation until the end of the Primary, likely to occur somewhere in the vicinity of mid-1980. The Bear Market which would follow should be of exceptional severity although relatively brief along the time span. Wave V of the Cycle Wave should begin in late 1981, probably be the most powerful move of the entire Bull Phase, and could conceivably take the F.T. 30 to several multiples of its current level given the laggard price action relative to the rate of inflation that has dogged stocks in the early 1970s.

TRADING INTERMEDIATE TERM MOVEMENTS

Of interest to the trader will be the Intermediate term moves within the Primary cycle. The correct application of the Wave Principle will help the more aggressive investor maximise his profits.

The first aspect that should be considered is the risk/reward potential of any particular move. The Wave Principle is the only forecasting device which is able to quantify this vital aspect of investment.

In the first instance, the Wave Principle trains its users to purchase at the terminal point of a decline and sell at the terminal point of a rise. Most other technical methods add up to little more than "trend chasing". After a move has been established the trader is then told to participate. This may be on a "breakout", or the penetrations of a trend line, or the completion of a "reversal pattern", etc. In this way, purchases and sales are made in a laggard fashion with the trader left with only a small portion of the total movement.

There have been severe criticisms levelled at technical methods in so much as these methods encourage trading and added costs. Usually one will find several profitable trades are wiped out by merely one loss when the conventional technical principles are used.

The Wave Principle differs greatly from these "trend chasing" methods. The object at all times is to attempt to effect purchases as close to a meaningful bottom as possible, and to effect sales as close to an important top as possible. By using the Wave Principle, we can anticipate approximately when and where such a top or bottom is likely to occur and adapt our trading strategy accordingly. I know of no other stock market device that can even aim at achieving this goal.

The first Intermediate term move that should be anticipated is that which will act to terminate the Intermediate cycle wave which began in January 1975. I have already established the likely time span and dimensions of this move. The pattern that should be anticipated is the "Zigzag" since the corrective down swing of the cycle will represent a 2 wave of the Primary Cycle.

Traders will liquidate their holdings in accordance with the strategy previously outlined. Aggressive traders will probably wish to engage in short selling for the initial "A" wave and the final "C" wave, covering and reversing their holdings during the "B" wave of the "Zigzag".

The opportunity offered after completion of the "Zigzag" will be one of the best of the overriding Bull move. When the "Zigzag" which acts to correct the Intermediate advance of January 1975-? is complete, the third wave of the Primary cycle will then commence. It is a tenet of the Wave Principle that the third wave of the cycle is usually the longest. The first wave of Wave 3 is likely to be exceptionally dynamic, therefore upon the final fifth wave of the "C" wave of the aforementioned "Zigzag" traders can enter the highest risk category of investment in order to maximise profits. These long positions should be held pending the completion of this third wave movement, likely to last at least 24 months.

Whereas short selling was recommended during the first corrective wave of the Primary cycle, this being the 2 wave, short selling is not recommended for the 4 wave of the cycle, but merely a liquidation of trading positions when the fifth Sub-Minuette wave, of the fifth Minuette wave, of the fifth Minute wave, of the fifth Minor Wave, of the fifth Intermediate wave of the third Primary Wave, is complete.

The 4 wave is likely to alternate in its complexity with the 2 wave. I have forecast the 2 wave as being a simple "A", "B", "C", "Zigzag". If the forecast is correct, the 4 wave of the primary move is likely to be complex, lending itself to a variety of patterns which could make timing somewhat difficult. In addition, should the 3 wave involve substantial strength, the 4 wave could well be very shallow in its extremities, and the margins entirely too small for effective short selling, both in time and amplitude.

Thus the Intermediate term trader would sell his holdings upon completion of Primary Wave 3, remain in cash or cash equivalents until the completion of Primary Wave 4, then re-enter the market for the fifth and final wave of the Primary, once again considering liquidations and short selling when the Primary is complete. When the Primary is complete, Wave 2 of the Cycle wave commences. An ideal short selling opportunity would be offered since the 2 wave of the Cycle Wave is likely to be greater in amplitude than any corrective action up to that point, and is also likely to take on the "Zigzag" form.

CONFIRMATION OF TERMINAL JUNCTURES

It was Elliott's intention to make his method as scientific as possible. However, in the final analysis, the difficulties imposed by the irregularity of wave development and the possible errors that can occur in counting leave effective use of the Wave Principle very much an art, as is the entire field of investment analysis. For this reason it is always wise to check and cross-check the forecasts that may be produced.

In all cases, the optimal opportunities will arrive at the completion of a five Wave Count whether in a Bull cycle or a Bear cycle. In a Bull cycle the five Wave Count will involve the completion of an upward impulse movement. In a Bear cycle, the five Wave Count will apply to the completion of the "C" wave which terminates the down move, excepting a few rare occasions which are readily identifiable (Triangles, Horizontals).

Whereas the five Wave Count will be the main criterion for establishing new positions, Elliott's rule "a corrective wave should not dip below the first key wave of the cycle which it is correcting" will offer the key to confirmation of a terminal juncture.

For example, the fifth wave of the Intermediate move will be completed when the fifth wave of the Sub-Minuette wave, of the fifth Minuette Wave, of the fifth wave of the Minute Wave, of the fifth wave of the Minor Wave is completed. In order to confirm the trend reversal action, one would first expect to see the Minute corrective action produce a down swing which falls below the first Sub-Minuette wave. This would then be followed by further declining action where the Minor Wave produces a move which falls below the first wave of the Minute move. Simply, as long as the corrective action of waves in progressively lower degrees is terminated above the first wave of the movement which is being corrected, the trend remains upward. As soon as the breach of this rule occurs, one can then assume a trend reversal is underway, particularly if such a trend reversal synchronises with five-wave movements of progressively higher degrees. In other words, should the corrective action which follows the fifth wave of a Sub-Minuette move result in a down swing that penetrates the first wave of that move, it is likely that a trend reversal is taking place in waves of a much higher degree, especially if such Sub-Minuette action also represents the fifth wave of a Minute movement which in turn is the fifth wave of a Minor movement, the fifth wave of the Minor movement also being the fifth wave of an Intermediate movement.

APPLICATIONS TO INDIVIDUAL SHARE PRICE MOVEMENTS

The examples used throughout the text up until now have all dealt with very broadly based stock market indices. The question arises, "Can the Wave Principle be used on the price action of individual shares?"

In the majority of cases, the Elliott Wave Principle will not be of much use with regard to individual share issues. It is of no value whatever in selection, and of marginal value with regard to timing. Elliott always kept in mind the basic principles of his philosophy and applied them in a reasonably consistent manner. His hypothesis was that the principle he "discovered" worked best when applied to the popular market averages rather than individual issues. This would appear to be logical in view of the emotional rationale behind the Wave Principle. The Wave Principle as seen in the broad movements of the stock market is the reflection of mass response to the stimuli of the averages. Accordingly, the greater the number that follow a particular market average, the more consistent will be the response. In New York, we have what many consider to be a mathematical monstrosity in the form of the antiquated D.J.30, yet this indicator is a far better *barometer* of the stock market than either the N.Y.S.E. Composite Index or the S&P 500 Index, despite the far greater number of shares in both of these latter indices.

When it came to the treatment of individual shares Elliott merely intimated that the best approach was to select issues which moved in harmony with the averages. Elliott also stressed marketability and soundness. His main recommendations were as follows:

1. First select the industrial groups that are performing in harmony with the averages.

2. Then select the shares that are moving in sympathy with the individual groups.

3. *Age of Shares*: According to Elliott, the life of a share has three stages:

    a. The first is the *youthful or experimental* stage during which such shares should be avoided as they have not been properly "seasoned".

b. The second is the *creative* stage. Shares that fall within this category have reached healthy development thus making them a desirable medium for trading providing they are thoroughly "seasoned".

c. The third or *grown-up* stage represents the period of fullest development. Dividends may be uniformly reliable and fluctuations narrow. For these reasons the certificates become lodged in portfolios and therefore the shares are less attractive for trading purposes.

4. Always choose shares that are constantly active, medium priced and seasoned leaders. A share that is frequently or occasionally inactive should be avoided for trading purposes because waves are not being registered. Inactivity clearly indicates that the share does not enjoy thorough distribution or that it has not yet reached the full stage of development. Furthermore, there are practical dangers in trying to apply the principle to the highflyers, because, typically, even one primary wave may go through a price rise of several hundred per cent. Intermediate moves would thus fluctuate wildly causing innumerable "whipsaws" if one tried to act on the price movement.

5. Diversify funds: i.e. employ more or less an equal amount of money in from five to ten companies and not more than one company in each group, for example:

TEXACO	DUPONT
BOEING	JOHNSON & JOHNSON
RAYTHEON	SAFEWAYS

In a broad sense, when using the Elliott Wave Principle as an aid to the timing of individual share purchases, the first thing one must watch out for is the five-wave pattern. Purchases should only be made in issues which have not yet completed their five wave patterns. It would also be imprudent to consider purchases in shares that are well along in their development of a fifth wave.

In this respect, the exact position of the market cycle may not be of much help. Elliott observed that individual issues will complete their own cycles, sometimes ahead of the market cycle, sometimes behind it. In Bull Markets each of the individual industrial groups will make their peaks at different times, rather like a fan. While many groups will perform in harmony with the averages throughout the Bull cycle, as many again will not. This phenomenon is just the opposite of what occurs in a Bear Market. At the bottom of a Bear Market, most industrial groups will reach their troughs in unison.

THE FINAL WORD

While Elliott's work has been available in the U.S. investment fraternity for some time it is yet to receive the attention it deserves. Most analysts will only adopt methods that are assimilable by other analysts, and clients… particularly institutional clients. Brokerage business is done through preconception rather than pre-cognition.

In any work of this kind one is bound to do less than justice to the job at hand. In order to have developed as complicated, yet logical, a mechanism as the Wave Principle, Elliott must have done practically nothing other than look at wave patterns in the stock market, subdivide them, classify them, superimpose other wave patterns on them, code, cross-check, etc., etc., in the dozen or so years he worked on his theory, from 1935 until his death in 1947.

Whether or not Elliott's "model" is the final word in technical stock market analysis is a question which will be argued for decades. What is true is that Elliott's Principle is a model of precision compared to the vagueness surrounding most other technical and chart principles which offer little of value to the intelligent investor.

Undoubtedly, the Wave Principle will be the subject of controversy among various schools of thought. It will lend itself to denigration by the anti-cyclical schools of thought. It will certainly be criticised by the anti-long-term-history school. It will be totally dismissed by the "random-walk" school, and it is unlikely to be greeted with cheer by the average "chartist" who is loath to accept any suggestion of inadequacies in his work, having been the target of heated criticism by practically all schools of investment thought for so long.

What most will not comprehend is that the Wave Principle lies far beyond all of that which has been mentioned. It is neither a cyclical theory, nor a theory based on historic repetition of price patterns. As such, the method has not and cannot be subject to the testing methods that have been used by the random walk theorists up to now, and it is decidedly set apart from the more simplistic chart methods.

The fundamentalists will certainly argue Elliott's hypothesis of never-ending growth. Most will say the "cult of equity" was pronounced dead in the early 1970s, and buried with the 1973-4 Bear Market. There is, however, a single rather secular term axiom that does apply here. Over extremely long runs in time there is the inescapable fact that money will devalue, and the prices of other things will thus increase. So whether we count the waves as Elliott suggests, or merely accept the inevitable as having no rhyme or reason, we will undoubtedly reach a higher plateau in the Dow-Jones Industrial Average than has ever been reached before, which in Elliott terms will complete the Grand Super Cycle.

I for one would certainly not wish to see the Dow-Jones Industrial Average at 36 billion times its current levels as the hyper-inflationists suggest could happen in the U.S., along the same lines as the German Stock Market in the 1920s. But even so, what may not be recognised is the fact that in foreign exchange terms, the German Stock Market Index did grow by 400 per cent during the period of hyper-inflation, and those who invested in equities did experience the benefit of the completion of the Super Cycle despite the decrease in value of practically everything else.

Should the Elliott forecasts prove substantially correct it is still doubtful if he will be remembered for them. The most emotionally unrewarding aspect of the Wave Principle is that one is trained to be bullish when most others are bearish, and bearish when practically the entire investment community is likely to be bullish. As such the Wave Principle lends itself to a self-feeding unpopularity... as do most successful investors in a collectivist society.

Appendix:
"The Wave Principle"

By R. N. Elliott

Original Publisher's Note:

D URING THE PAST seven or eight years, publishers of financial magazines and organizations in the investment advisory field have been virtually flooded with "systems" for which their proponents have claimed great accuracy in forecasting stock market movements. Some of them appeared to work for a while. It was immediately obvious that others had no value whatever. All have been looked upon by THE FINANCIAL WORLD with great scepticism. But after the investigation of Mr. R. N. Elliott's Wave Principle THE FINANCIAL WORLD became convinced that a series of articles on this subject would be interesting and instructive to its readers. To the individual reader it is left the determination of the value of the Wave Principle as a working tool in market forecasting, but it is believed that it should prove at least a useful check upon conclusions based on economic considerations.

The Editors of The Financial World

INTRODUCING "THE WAVE PRINCIPLE"

Since the beginning of time, rhythmic regularity has been the law of creation. Gradually man has acquired knowledge and power from studying the various manifestations of this law. The effects of the law are discernible in the behaviour of the tides, the heavenly bodies, cyclones, day and night, even life and death! This rhythmic regularity is called a cycle.

Historical Significance

The first great advance in the scientific application of the law was made in the time of Columbus by Leonardo da Vinci in his illuminating study of the behavior of waves. Other great men followed with special applications: Halley with this comet, Bell with sound waves, Edison with electrical waves, Marconi with radio waves, and still others with waves of psychology, cosmic waves, television, etc. One thing in common that all these waves or forms of energy have is their cyclical behavior or ability to repeat themselves indefinitely. This cyclical behavior is characterized by two forces – one building up and the other tearing down. Today Hitler is said to be timing his conquests in accordance with this natural law as interpreted in the movement of the stars – but the destructive forces are accumulating and at the proper time will become dominant – completing the cycle.

Because of this phenomenon of repetition or rhythmic recurrence, it is possible to apply the lesson learned from other manifestations of the law in a very practical and profitable way. The trade cycle and the bull and bear movements of the stock market are also governed by the same natural law. Some fifty years ago Charles Dow through his observations of the important changes in the stock market gradually built up the Dow Theory, which now is accepted in many quarters as having special forecasting significance. Since Dow's studies, the store of information regarding market transactions has been greatly multiplied, and important and valuable new forecasting inferences can be drawn from certain behavior.

Through a long illness the writer had the opportunity to study the available information concerning stock market behavior. Gradually the wild, senseless and apparently uncontrollable changes in prices from year to year, from month to month, or from day to day, linked themselves into a law-abiding rhythmic pattern of waves. This pattern seems to repeat itself over and over again. With knowledge of this law or phenomenon (that I have called the Wave Principle) it is possible to measure and forecast the various trends and corrections (minor, intermediate, major and even movements of a still greater degree) that go to complete a great cycle.

FIGURE 1

This phenomenon is disclosed in Figure 1. The full wave or progressive phase of the cycle consists of five impulses: three moving forward and two moving downward. Waves 1, 3 and 5 are in the direction of the main trend. Wave 2 corrects Wave 1 – and Wave 4 corrects Wave 3. Usually the three forward movements are in approximately parallel planes; this may also be true of Waves 2 and 4.

FIGURE 2

Each of the three primary waves that together make a completed movement is divided into five waves of the next smaller or intermediate degree. This subdivision is shown in Figure 2. Note carefully that there are five smaller or intermediate waves making up the Primary Wave 1, five in Primary Wave 3, and five in Primary Wave 5. The Primary Wave 2 corrects the completed Primary Wave 1 consisting of five intermediate waves; Wave 4 in turn corrects the five intermediate waves that make up Primary Wave 3.

FIGURE 3

Each intermediate forward wave is in turn divided into five minor waves as shown in Figure 3. When the fifth minor wave of the fifth intermediate phase of the fifth primary movement has spent its force, a formidable top has been constructed. Upon completion of a movement of this magnitude, the destructive forces become dominant; the primary trend turns downward and a bear market is in progress long before the economic, political or financial reasons for the change in outlook are clearly apparent.

THE WAVE PRINCIPLE: PART II

In the preceding discussion of the Wave Principle as applied to the forecasting of stock price movements, it was pointed out that a completed movement consists of five waves, and that a set of five waves of one degree completes the first wave of the next higher degree. When Wave 5 of any degree has been completed, there should occur a correction that will be more severe than any previous correction in the cyclical movement.

Completed Movement

The rhythm of the corrective phases is different from that of the waves moving in the direction of the main trend. These corrective vibrations, or Waves 2 and 4, are each made up of *three* lesser waves, whereas progressive waves (1, 3 and 5) are each composed of *five* smaller impulses. In Figure 4, the completed movement is shown, being identical to Figure 3 except that Waves 2 and 4 of the "zigzag" pattern are shown in greater detail. These Waves 2 and 4 are thus shown to consist each of three component phases but as these two waves are also "completed movements", they are also characterized by *five-wave* impulses; that is the "a" and "c" phases (the first and third movements of the correction) are also each composed of five smaller waves, while "b" (the correction of the correction) is composed of three lesser waves. This question of corrections will require more extended discussion later on, as some forms and types are so complicated in structure that their presentation at this stage might be confusing.

FIGURE 4

The student using the Wave Principle to forecast price changes does not require confirmation by a companion average, inasmuch as the

Principle applies to individual stocks, to various groups (steel, rails, utilities, coppers, oils, etc.), and also to commodities and the various "averages", such as those of Dow-Jones, Standard Statistics, *New York Times*, *New York Herald Tribune*, the *Financial Times* of London, etc. At any given time it will be found that some stocks are advancing and others are declining; but the great majority of individual stocks will be following the same pattern at the same time. It is for this reason that the wave pattern of the "averages" will correctly reflect the cyclical position of the market as a whole. The larger the number of stocks in an average, the more sharply outlined the wave impressions will be. This means that if stocks are widely distributed among a large number of individuals, the response to cyclical influences will be registered more definitely and rhythmically than if the distribution is limited.

Price Ranges Used

No reliance can be placed on "closings", daily or weekly. It is the highest and lowest ranges that guide the subsequent course of the cycle. In fact it was only due to the establishment and publication by Dow-Jones of the "daily range" in 1928 and of "hourly range" in 1932, that sufficient reliable data became available to establish the rhythmic recurrence of the phenomenon that I have called the Wave Principle. It is the series of actual "travels" by the market, hourly, daily and weekly, that reveal the rhythmic forces in their entirety. The "closings" do not disclose the full story, and it is for this reason (lack of detailed data) that the phase-by-phase course of the London stock market is more difficult to predict than the New York market.

The complete measurement of the length of a wave is therefore its continuous travel between two corrections of the same or greater degree. The length of a wave of the lowest degree is its travel in one direction without any sort of correction even in the hourly record. After two corrections have appeared in the hourly record, the movement then enters its fifth and last stage, or third impulse. So-called "resistance" levels and other technical considerations have but little value in forecasting or measuring the length or duration of these waves.

Outside Influences

As the Wave Principle forecasts the different phases of a cycle, the experienced student will find that current news or happenings, or even decrees or acts of government, seem to have but little effect, if any, upon the course of the cycle. It is true that sometimes unexpected news or sudden events, particularly those of a highly emotional nature, may extend or curtail the length of travel between corrections, but the number of waves or underlying rhythmic regularity of the market remains constant. It even seems to be more logical to conclude that the cyclical derangement of trade, bringing widespread social unrest, is the cause of wars, rather than that cycles are produced by wars.

THE WAVE PRINCIPLE: PART III

Because, after the Fifth Wave of an advancing movement has been completed, the correction will be more severe than any yet experienced in the cycle, it is desirable to determine beforehand where the top of this wave will be. With such knowledge, the investor can take necessary steps to assume a defensive policy and convert profits into cash under the most favourable market conditions. He will also be in a strong position to repurchase with confidence when the correction has run its course.

The previous article stated that "The complete measurement of the length of a wave is therefore its continuous travel between two corrections of the same or greater degree." By repeatedly measuring the length of these waves as they develop, under a method known as channelling, it is possible to determine at the time of completion of Wave 4 approximately where Wave 5 should "top".

Figure 5 shows a normal completed movement or "cycle", in which Waves 1, 3 and 5 each have approximately the same length. Forecasting the ultimate movement by the channelling methods must wait until Waves 1 and 2 have been completed. At such time it is possible to ascertain the "base line" for the lower limits of the channel by extending a straight line from the starting point of Wave 1 through the stopping point of Wave 2. This is shown in Fig. 6. Wave 3, normally parallel to Wave 1, should end in the approximate vicinity of the tentative or dashed upper line of the channel.

FIGURES 5 & 6

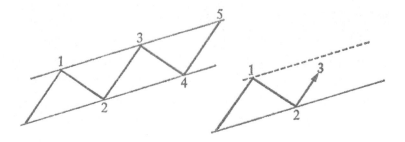

The tentative upper line is drawn parallel to the base line from the top of Wave 1 and extended forward. But conditions may be so favorable that Wave 3 takes on temporary strength and exceeds the normal theoretical expectation, as shown in Fig. 7.

FIGURES 7 & 8

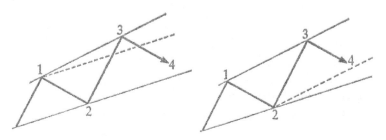

When Wave 3 has ended, the actual upper channel line is drawn from the top of Wave 1 through the top of Wave 3. And for forecasting the bottom of Wave 4 reaction, a tentative or dashed line is drawn from the bottom of Wave 2 parallel to the actual Wave 1-Wave 3 upper channel line. In Figure 8 the theoretical expectancy for termination of Wave 4 is shown, as well as the actual termination.

With the second reaction, or Wave 4, terminated, the final and all-important channeling step can be taken. The base line of the channel is extended across the stopping points of the two reactionary phases (Waves 2 and 4), and a parallel upper line is drawn across the top of Wave 3. Wave 1 is disregarded entirely, unless Wave 3 was exceptionally strong. When the base and upper parallel lines are drawn as suggested, the approximate termination of Wave 5 will be forecast, as shown in Figure 9.

FIGURE 9

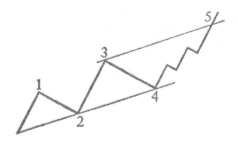

This channelling method is, of course, subordinate in importance to the rhythm of the various phases that make up the completed movement. Waves 1, 3 and 5 should each be composed of five waves of the next lower degree. Theoretically Wave 5 should wind up at about the intersection with the upper parallel lie drawn as above described. Sometimes, however, Wave 5 develops excessive strength. Patterns in which this "throw-over" should occur will be discussed in subsequent articles.

THE WAVE PRINCIPLE: PART IV

A completed price movement has been shown to consist of five waves, with the entire movement representing the first wave of the next larger degree. By classifying the degree of the various phases, it is possible to determine the relative position of the market at all times as well as the economic changes that should follow.

The longest reliable record of American stock prices is the Axe-Houghton Index (published in *The New York Times Annalist*) dating from 1854. Long range forecasting under the Wave Principle must therefore start with the completion of the bear market that terminated in 1857. The great tidal movement that commenced in 1857 and ended on November 28, 1928 (the orthodox top) represents one wave of a cycle of the largest degree. Whether this extended movement was the First, Third or Fifth wave of the *Grand Super Cycle* necessarily depends upon what happened previous to 1857. By breaking the historic wave down into its component series of five-wave movements, and by breaking in turn the fifth wave of the next smaller degree into its five waves, the student will have actual examples of the various degrees that markets traverse. To avoid confusion in classifying the various degrees of market movements, it is suggested that the names and symbols devised below be used in their respective order:

Degree of Movement	Symbol and Wave No.	Duration
Grand Super Cycle	gsc I (?)··	1857-1928
	sc I··	1857-1864
	sc II··	1864-1877
Super Cycle··········	sc III··	1877-1881
	sc IV··	1881-1896
	sc V··	1896-1928
	c I··	1896-1899
	c II··	1899-1907
Cycle··········	c III··	1907-1909
	c IV··	1909-1921
	c V··	1921-1928
	((I))··	June, 1921-Mar., 1923
	((II))··	Mar., 1923-May, 1924
Primary··········	((III))··	May, 1924-Nov., 1925
	((IV))··	Nov., 1925-Mar., 1926
	((V))··	Mar., 1926-Nov., 1928

Intermediate··	(I)-(V)	**Price movements**
Minor··	I-V	**illustrating the**
Minute··	1-5	**Intermediate and**
Minuette··	A-E	**smaller degrees will**
Sub-Minuette··	a-e	**be discussed in**
		subsequent articles.

The longest of these waves lasted for over 70 years and included a long series of "bull" and "bear" markets. But it is the combination of the smaller hourly, daily and weekly rhythms that complete and measure the important *Intermediate* and *Primary* cycles that are of great practical importance to every investor.

When the Dow-Jones industrial averages reached 295.62 on November 28, 1928, the price movement completed the fifth *Minuette* impulse of the fifth *Minute* wave of the fifth *Minor* phase of the fifth *Intermediate* movement of the fifth *Primary* trend in the fifth *Cycle* of the fifth *Super Cycle* in Wave 1, 3 or 5 of the *Grand Super Cycle*. For that reason, although the actual top of 386.10 was not reached until September 3, 1929, the point reached on November 28, 1928, is designated as the "orthodox" top. This may sound confusing to most readers, but the patterns in which "irregular tops" higher than "orthodox tops" occur will be discussed in due course.

THE WAVE PRINCIPLE: PART V

The scope and duration of any price movement are influenced by what happened in the previous cycle of similar or larger degree. The movement that started in 1896 and took 33 years to complete, culminating on September 3, 1929, at 386.10, was so dynamic that the corrective bear cycle was correspondingly severe.

Orderly Decline

Within less than three years, prices were reduced to 10.5 per cent of the peak level. Despite its high speed, the downward course of the bear cycle followed a well-defined and rhythmic pattern of waves. Furthermore, it kept within the limits of the pre-measured channel. It was, therefore, possible to determine beforehand approximately where the bear market would end and the new bull market begin. Because of the amplitude of the previous cycles, the new bull market would necessarily be of a large degree, lasting for years. When taking a position for such a large movement, the long term investor would be warranted in maintaining his investments until the end of the fifth major wave was in measurable sight. From that point he should be extremely careful.

FIGURE 10

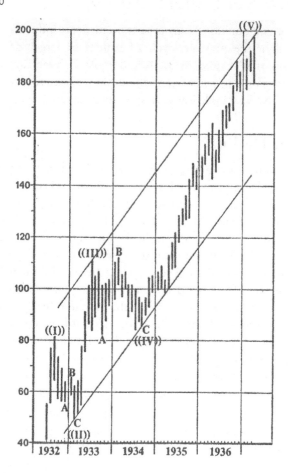

Phases of the Primary Movement, 1932-1937

Wave ((I)) from 40.56 July 8, 1932 to completion of Wave ((V)) at 195.59 on March 10, 1937. (Dow-Jones Industrial Monthly Averages)

Wave		From				To			
((I))	40.56	July	8,	1932	–	81.39	Sept	8,	1932
((II))	81.39	Sept	8,	1932	–	49.68	Feb	27,	1933
A	81.39	Sept	8,	1932	–	55.04	Dec	3,	1932
B	55.04	Dec	3,	1932	–	65.28	Jan	11,	1933
C	65.28	Jan	11,	1933	–	49.68	Feb	27,	1933
((III))	49.68	Feb	27,	1933	–	110.53	July	18,	1933
((IV))	110.53	July	18,	1933	–	84.58	July	26,	1934
A	110.53	July	18,	1933	–	82.20	Oct	21,	1933
B	82.20	Oct	21,	1933	–	111.93	Feb	5,	1934
C	111.93	Feb	5,	1934	–	84.58	Feb	26,	1934
(V)	84.58	July	26,	1934	–	195.59	Mar	10,	1937

Previous discussions have dealt with the fundamental theory of the Wave Principle. It is now appropriate to show the application of the theory to an actual market. Figure 10, the completed five-wave movement of the extreme monthly price ranges of the Dow-Jones industrial averages from July 8, 1932 to March 10, 1937, is charted arithmetically. The series of minuette, minute, minor and intermediate waves all resolved themselves – in the monthly, weekly, daily and hourly records – to form and complete each of the five Primary waves. Waves ((I)), ((III)) and ((V)) were each composed of five lesser or intermediate degrees. The corrective Waves ((II)) and ((IV)) were each composed of three distinct phases, as shown by the A-B-C pattern. The extent and duration of each important phase are shown in the accompanying table.

When Wave ((IV)) is finished and Wave ((V)) is under way, much closer attention to the market is required. Accordingly the channel (see Part III, FW, April. 19) was carefully noted. A base line was drawn from the bottom of Wave ((II)) through the bottom of Wave ((IV)), and an upper line parallel thereto was extended forward from the top of Wave ((III)). See the accompanying table and chart.

Bearish Indication?

In November 1936, immediately after the President was reelected by an overwhelming majority vote, external conditions appeared to be so favourable for the bull market that it was extremely difficult to think of being bearish. Yet according to the Wave Principle, the bull market even then was in its final stage. The long term movement that started in 1932 had by November 12, 1936, reached 185.52, and the various five-wave advances of the preceding 53 months were in the culminating stage of the Primary degree. Note how close the price level was to the upper part of the channel at that time. Yet it required another four months to complete the pattern.

The final and relatively insignificant wave, necessary to confirm that the end was at hand, developed during the week ended Wednesday, March 10, 1937. In that week both the industrial and rail averages moved forward on huge volume to a moderately higher recovery level and, according to one of the most widely followed market theories thereby "reaffirmed that the major trend was *upward*".

The industrials reached 195.59 – compared with the November 1929, panic bottom of 195.35 and the February, 1931, rally top of 196.96. In that week the advancing prices met the top of the channel. The President's remarks about prices for copper and steel being too high did not take place until April, and by that time the bear movement was well under way.

THE WAVE PRINCIPLE: PART VI

In the 1932-1937 Primary bull movement (see Fig. 10, Part V, FW, May 3) Waves ((I)) and ((III)) ran at high speed. Naturally they terminated in a short time. But Wave ((V)) was so gradual and orderly that it lasted longer than the time interval required for the previous four waves combined. In the discussion of this movement, it was stated that by November, 1936, it was evident that the bull market was in an extremely advanced stage, but that it required another four months to complete the pattern. Although the largest phases of the Fifth Primary were in the culminating stage, the smallest component phases (Minuette, etc.) were still developing.

Figure 11 illustrates how the fifth wave of an important degree becomes extended by the development of five waves of the next smaller degree, and five more of a still smaller degree. Thus, an Intermediate trend will end on the fifth Sub-Minuette impulse of the fifth Minuette wave of the fifth Minute phase of the fifth Minor movement of the fifth Intermediate swing. Note that as Wave (V) advances, the corrections tend to become smaller and of shorter duration. Compare with 1935-1937. The termination of a fifth wave marks the point at which an entire movement of the same degree is to be corrected by a reverse movement of a similar degree.

FIGURE 11

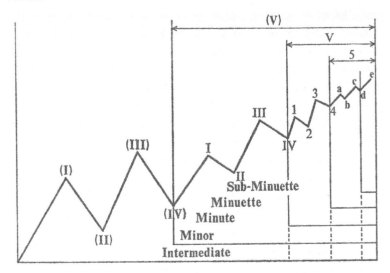

Confusion in the identification of the waves of the smaller degrees, developing toward the end of the fifth wave of the important degree, is sometimes caused by "throw-overs". A throw-over is a penetration, in an advancing movement of the upper parallel line of the channel (see Part III, FW, Apr. 19), and in a declining movement of the lower parallel line of the channel. Volume tends to rise on a throw-over, and should be very heavy as applied to the fifth Intermediate wave of a Primary movement. Failure of the fifth wave of any degree to penetrate the channel line, accompanied by indications of a sustained decline, is a warning of weakness. The extent of the weakness depends upon the degree of the wave. Sometimes, such weakness furnishes a new base for the recommencement of the fifth wave. Throw-overs are also caused by the scale of the chart study of the movement. They are more likely to occur in an advancing movement on arithmetic scales, and in declining movements on logarithmic scales.

Sometimes the fifth wave will "stretch" – that is, deploy or spread out. The fifth wave, instead of preceding in the normal one-wave pattern of the same degree as the movement as a whole, simply stretches or sub-divides into five waves of lower degree. In rhythmic forecasting, this stretching applies to the fifth wave itself, rather than to the terminating cycle of which it is a part. Such spreading out is a characteristic of markets that are unusually strong (or weak, if a down movement). An example of stretching occurred in the 1921-1928 upswing, representing the culmination of a 72-year advance.

THE WAVE PRINCIPLE: PART VII

The rhythm of corrective movements is the most difficult feature of the Wave Principle. Intensive study of the correction will sometimes be necessary in order to determine the position of the market and the outlook. Mastery of the subject, however, should prove extremely profitable. All corrections are characterized by *three* broad waves, but the detail and extent can vary considerably, and thus different patterns are formed. Various factors (time, rate of speed, extent of previous movement, volume, news items, etc.) tend to influence and shape the corrective pattern. Based on the writer's market research and experience, there appear to be four main types or patterns of corrections. These types have been designated as (1) Zig-zag, (2) Flat, (3) Irregular, and (4) Triangle. Discussion of the Triangle, in its various forms, must be presented in a separate article. The other three forms are diagramed in Figures 12, 13 and 14.

Small corrections that run their course in a comparatively short time are exemplified in Figure 12. Corrections of a larger degree are described in Figure 13. Figure 14 affords a diagram of the market action when the Primary or Intermediate trends turn downward. Some of these corrections, particularly those of the Irregular type, may extend over a period of years and embrace movements that are commonly mistaken for "bull markets".

FIGURES 12, 13 & 14

Zig-Zag	Flat	Irregular types

The three-wave or A-B-C formations that characterize the Zig-zag, Flat and Irregular corrections are clearly shown in the accompanying diagrams. The Zig-zag type was discussed briefly in Part II (Fig. 4, FW, Apr. 12). It differs from other corrections in that both the first and third waves (A and C) are composed of five smaller vibrations. The second ("B") wave of Zig-zag corrections is composed of three impulses. Sometimes, in a high-speed movement, the first leg ("A") may appear continuous, and resort to the smaller or hourly studies may be necessary to detect the flow.

The first and second waves of both Flats and Irregulars each consist of *three* vibrations of a degree smaller than that of the previous movement. Of the three movements making up the second or "B" phase of both Flats and Irregulars, the first and third ("a" and "c") are each composed of *five* still smaller impulses. In a Flat all of the three waves have approximately the same length.

An Irregular correction is distinguished by the fact that the second or "B" wave advances to a secondary top higher than the orthodox top established in the primary movement. Liquidation in the third or "C" wave is therefore usually more intensive than in the first phase. Normally "C" terminates below the bottom of "A", although there are instances of "C", the third phase, being abbreviated. In the larger and important corrections, such as Primary and Intermediate, the "C" or third phase of the Irregular correction may consist of *three smaller five-wave sets*, as shown in Figure 14.

By analyzing and placing the type of correction that is being experienced, the student has a basis for determining both the extent of the correction, and the extent of the following movement. Channeling (see Part III, FW, Apr. 19) can help in determining the extent. The application of these corrective patterns will be shown and discussed in subsequent articles.

THE WAVE PRINCIPLE: PART VIII

Triangular corrections are protracted trend hesitations. The main movement may have gone too far and too fast in relation to the slower economic processes, and prices proceed to mark time until the underlying forces catch up. Triangles have lasted as long as nine months and have been as short as seven hours. There are two classes of triangles, horizontal and diagonal. These are shown in Figures 15 and 16.

The four types of horizontal triangles are (1) Ascending, (2) Descending, (3) Symmetrical, and (4) the rare Reverse Symmetrical. In the last named the apex is the beginning of the triangular correction. In the other forms the apex is the end of the correction, which, however, may terminate before the apex is actually reached.

All triangles contain five waves or legs, each of which is composed of not more than three lesser waves. Outlines that do not conform to this definition fall outside of the law of the Wave Principle. All waves in a triangle must be part of a movement in one direction; otherwise, the "triangle" is only a coincidence.

FIGURES 15, 16 & 17

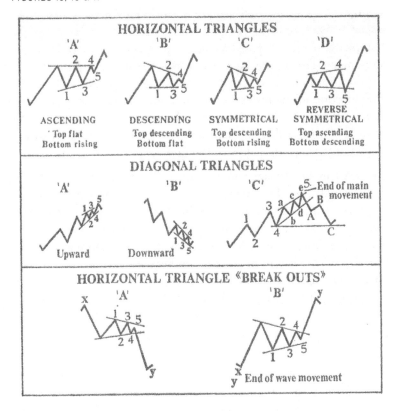

The entire travel within the triangle represents a wave of the main movement. The horizontal triangle occurs as Wave 2 or Wave 4. If it occurs as Wave 2, the main movement will have only three waves. At the conclusion of a horizontal triangle, the market will resume the trend that was interrupted by the triangle, and the direction of that trend will be the same as that of triangular Wave 2. The "break-out" from the horizontal triangle (in the direction of triangular Wave 2) will usually be fast and represent the final wave of the main movement, and be followed by reversal of the trend. The extent of the "break-out" will usually approximate the distance between the widest parts of the triangle. Diagrams A and B, Fig. 17, illustrate the "break-out" from horizontal triangles.

Diagonal triangles are either (1) upward or (2) downward. They can occur as either Wave 3 or Wave 4 of the main movement. Usually they occur as Wave 5, and are preceded by four main waves. But the completion of the diagonal triangle represents the end of the main movement. The second wave within the diagonal triangle will be in the direction opposite to that of the main movement, and will indicate the direction of the reversal to follow conclusion of the triangle. At the conclusion of the fifth wave in this form of triangle, the rapid reversal of trend will usually return the market to about the level from which the triangle started. See diagram C, Fig. 16.

Triangles are not apparent in all studies. Sometimes they will appear in the weekly scale, but will not be visible in the daily. Sometimes they are present in, say, *The New York Times* average and not in another average. Thus, the broad and important movement from October, 1937, to February, 1938, formed a triangle in the Standard Statistics weekly range, but was not visible in other averages; the second wave of this triangle pointed downward; the fifth wave culminated on February 23; the drastic March break followed.

THE WAVE PRINCIPLE: PART IX

The "extension," though not frequent is one of the most important market phenomena measurable by The Wave Principle. In an extension the length (and degree) of the wave becomes much larger than normal. It may occur as a part of Wave 1 or 3, but is usually a part of Wave 5 of the main movement. The extended movement is composed of the normal five-wave phase, followed by a three-wave retracing correction, and then by a second advancing movement in three phases. Of the normal five waves, the fifth vibration is usually the largest and most dynamic of the series – thus becoming, in effect, an extension of the extension.

A warning of the approach of this dynamic phase of Wave 5 is conveyed when Waves 1 and 3 are short and regular and confined with the channel, and when the first corrective vibration of the extension is completed near the top of the channel. The length of important extensions may be several times the breadth of the original channel.

Channelling is also useful in measuring the travel of the extension. Thus, in Figures 18 and 19, the line "b-d" represents the base line, and the dashed upper parallel line "c-e" measures the normal expectancy for the "first top" of the extension.

The completion of the normal or first waves of an extension is never the end of the cyclical movement, but does constitute a distinct warning that the bull cycle is approaching an end, as only two move broad waves (one down and one up) would fully reflect the maximum force of the bull market.

FIGURES 18 & 19

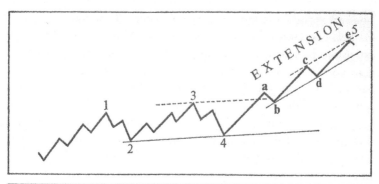

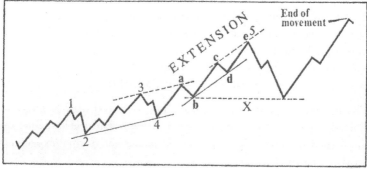

After the first five waves of the extension have been completed, a severe correction (that is usually in three waves, but may be triangular) sets in. This correction becomes Wave A of an irregular cyclical correction. Wave A generally carries the market down (breaking the extension channel) to about the beginning of the extension, although a protracted period of backing and filling may serve to mitigate the severity of this corrective phase. The dashed line marked "X" in Figure 19 indicates the average expectancy for the completion of Wave A.

When Wave A has been completed, the main or cyclical movement is resumed in three broad phases that carry the market into new high ground – even though "e" in Figures 18 and 19 may have been the "orthodox top" of a major or primary bull movement. But this new top, or "irregular top," is the final high point for the bull market. This three-wave advancing phase becomes Wave B of the irregular cyclical correction.

The completion of Wave B marks the beginning of Wave C of the irregular cyclical correction, that in this phase is a bear market of major importance. Wave C should carry the market down in five fast waves to about the bottom of Primary Wave IV of the preceding bull movement. Example: following the dynamic extension in 1928; Wave A, down from November to December 1928; Wave B, upward to September, 1929; Wave C, downward to July, 1932.

Extensions also occur in bear markets. Thus, the five waves of an extension were completed October 19, 1937, with the market reaching 115.83; followed, in this case, by a broad triangular correction (instead of the irregular A-B-C pattern) covering a period of four months, eventually reaching 97.46 on March 31, 1938. Wave 2 of this triangular correction was in the same direction as the downward cyclical trend.

A tremendous extension occurred in commodity price movements, particularly that of electrolyte copper, in the spring of 1937. In individual stocks, the "orthodox top" of International Harvester was reached at 111-112 in January, 1937; Wave A, in a backing and filling movement that reduced the severity of the correction, carried the stock to 109 in April; Wave B reached a new cyclical top of 120 in August (the general market topped in March), and Wave C brought the stock down to about 53 in November.

THE WAVE PRINCIPLE: PART X

Following the completion of the bull market from 1932-1937 (see Figure 10, FW, May 3, 1939), a three-phase cyclical correction was in order. The first phase should and did consist of five large waves. The first phase of the correction was the decline that ran from 195.59 (Dow-Jones industrial averages) on March 10, 1937, to 94.46 on March 31, 1938. The accompanying Figure 20 shows the weekly range of the market during this period, on an arithmetic scale. Despite the highly emotional nature that prevailed at certain stages, the rhythmic forecasting principle continued to function. The minute details registered in the daily and hourly patterns are, of course, not entirely visible in the weekly range. For this reason, the essential details or price and time of the five big waves making up this first cyclical phase are given:

> Cyclical Wave (A) – from 195.59 on March 10, 1937, to 163.31 on June 17, 1937.
>
> Cyclical Wave (B) – from 163.31 on June 17, 1937, to 190.38 on August 14, 1937.
>
> Cyclical Wave (C) – from 190.38 on August 14, 1937, to 115.83 on October 19, 1937.
>
> Cyclical Wave (D) – from 115.83 on October 19, 1937, to 132.86 on February 23, 1938.
>
> Cyclical Wave (E) – from 132.86 on February 23, 1938, to 97.46 on March 31, 1938.

FIGURE 20

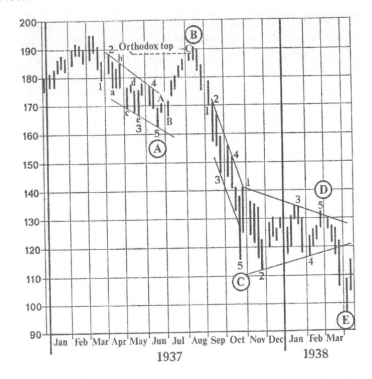

Cyclical Wave (A) was composed of five minor waves, as follows:

1 – 195.59 on March 10 to 179.28 on March 22.
2 – 179.28 on March 22 to 187.99 on March 31.
3 – 187.99 on March 31 to 166.20 on May 18.
4 – 166.20 on May 18 to 175.66 on June 5.
5 – 175.66 on June 5 to 163.31 on June 17.

Wave 3 in Cyclical Wave (A) was composed of five vibrations.

Cyclical Wave (B) was composed of three waves, and an "irregular top":

A – 163.31 on June 17 to 170.46 on June 24.
B – 170.46 on June 24 to 166.11 on June 29.
C – 166.11 on June 29 to 187.31 on August 4.

The "irregular top" was completed on August 11, 1937, forecasting a severe cyclical decline.

Cyclical Wave (C) was composed of five large waves, with an "extension" developing in the fifth wave. Had it not been for this extension, the normal completion of the first phase of the cyclical correction would probably have been in the neighbourhood of 135-140. The analysis of Wave (C) is as follows:

> 1 – 190.38 on August 14, 1937, to 175.09 on August 27, 1937.
> 2 – 175.09 on August 27, 1937, to 179.10 on August 31, 1937.
> 3 – 179.10 on August 31, 1937, to 154.94 on Sept. 13, 1937.
> 4 – 154.94 on Sept. 13, 1937, to 157.12 on Sept. 30, 1937.
> 5 – 157.12 on Sept. 30, 1937, to 115.83 on Oct. 19, 1937.

In cyclical Wave (C), there were three "sets" of five vibrations in each downward trend, with the first, third and fifth minor waves each being composed of five impulses. Wave 4 was a fairly important upward correction, in the familiar A-B-C formation. The "extension" that developed in the fifth vibration of Wave 5 indicated that (1) the ground thus lost would be immediately recovered, (2) that the secondary decline would carry the market into new low ground for the cyclical correction, (3) that following this secondary decline, the normal protracted period of backing and filling might form a triangle, with the final dawn thrust completing the first phase of the cyclical correction, and (4) that a very substantial recovery would follow, in at least five large waves – thus forecasting the 1938 March-November "bull market."

Cyclical Wave (D), as indicated by the "extension" that occurred in Wave (C), was composed of a huge triangle:

Triangle Wave 1 – in three vibrations, from 115.83 on October 19, 1937, to 141.22 on October 29 as follows:

> A – 115.83 on October 19 to 137.82 on October 21.
> B – 137.82 on October 21 to 124.56 on October 25.
> C – 124.56 on October 25 to 141.22 on October 29.
> 2 – 141.22 on October 29, 1937, to 112.54 on November 23.
> 3 – 112.54 on November 23 to 134.95 on January 12, 1938.

4 – 134.95 on January 12 to 117.13 on February 4.
5 – 117.13 on February 4 to 132.86 on February 23.

None of the "legs" in this triangle was composed of more than three waves. Following the completion of the fifth wave in the triangle, the downward movement of the cyclical correction was resumed.

Cyclical Wave (E) was composed of five lesser waves, as follows:

1 – 132.86 on February 23 to 121.77 on March 13.
2 – 121.77 on March 12 to 127.44 on March 15.
3 – 127.44 on March 15 to 112.78 on March 23.
4 – 112.78 on March 23 to 114.37 on March 25.
5 – 114.37 on March 25 to 97.46 on March 31.

The first large phase of the cyclical correction of the 1932-1937 bull market was thus finally completed, and the market was ready for the second important upward phase of the cyclical correction. This correction extinguished 63.3 per cent of the 155.03 points recovered in the 1932-1937 movement.

THE WAVE PRINCIPLE: PART XI

In using the Wave Principle as a medium for forecasting price movements, the student should recognize that there are cycles within cycles, and that each such cycle or sub-cycle must be studied and correctly placed in respect to the broad underlying movement. These sub-cyclical or corrective phases in a bull market are often important enough to be mistaken for "bear markets." The strong but sub-cyclical correction from March 31, 1938, to November 12, 1938, had a "bull pattern" of five important waves making up its first phase, and was (and still is) regarded by many as a real bull market. Broadly speaking, extended rallies or corrections of bear cycles are composed of three phases, and this is also true of extensive bearish corrections of bull movements.

Wave Characteristics

The character of the waves making up an extended movement is affected by a number of factors that may seem irrelevant to the inexperienced. Examination of any completed movement seems to support the fatalistic theory that the extent or objective of the price movement is fixed or predetermined. The time of the entire cycle is also possibly fixed, but the time of the component phases appears to be variable. The variations in the time cycle appear to be governed by the speed or rate of the price movement, and vice versa. Thus, if the market movement has been violent and rapid in one phase, the next corresponding phase is likely to show a marked slowing down in speed. Example: The first primary wave of the 1932-1937 bull cycle advanced 40 points or 100 per cent in 9 weeks, averaging 4.4 points per week. The second bull phase advanced 60 points or 120 per cent in 20 weeks, averaging 3 points per week. The third or final phase crept forward 110 points or 130 per cent in 138 weeks, averaging 0.8 point per week. High speed at the end of long movements usually generates similar speed in the first wave of the reversal: compare the March, 1938, downward movement with the following April reversal.

At certain stages volume seems to play an important part in the price movement, and volume itself will expand or contract to help control and complete the price cycle. Study of the time cycle and volume cycles is sometimes distinctly helpful in clarifying the position of the price spiral. Volume tends to increase in the third wave of the cycle, and to maintain about the same activity in the fifth wave. As the bottom of the volume cycle is approached, erratic price changes in high priced stocks or inactive stocks with thin markets, can distort the small waves in the trend of the averages to such an extent as to create temporary uncertainties. But these waves of volume are also useful in determining the extent and time for completion of price phases, and also in determining the time and direction and even the speed of the following movement. This is especially true in fast swinging markets like those that characterized 1938. The best results therefore will follow from correlation of the volume and time cycles with the component phases of the broad price movement, as the price patterns and all degrees of volume are governed by precisely the same Wave Principle phenomenon.

To maintain a proper perspective, the student should chart at least two and preferably more broad averages, using the weekly range, the daily range, and the hourly record, and showing the accompanying volume. The weekly range should be sufficient properly to evaluate the broad changes in trend, but the monthly range studies will also undoubtedly appeal to many investors. The daily range, by affording close observation of the smaller changes, is essential in correct interpretation of the cyclical progression, and is quite necessary for determining the precise time of important reversals in trend.

Critical Points

The minute changes recorded in the hourly study not only afford valuable and extensive material for practice in wave interpretation, but are especially useful in times when the market is moving at such high speed that the pattern is not clearly registered in the longer-time charts. Thus, the small triangle that appeared in the hourly record of October 1937, signalled an immediate acceleration or extension of the downward movement; the dynamic October 18-19 "panic" followed. At other critical points the hourly study has also proved valuable, as in locating the "orthodox top" before the final irregular top, thus selecting the time for strategic liquidation near the crest. As the first hourly phase following the break in March 1938 developed in five-minute waves, it thus afforded a strong confirmation that the important trend had actually changed.

THE WAVE PRINCIPLE: PART XII

Previous articles have discussed the theory of The Wave Principle and its application to broad market movements. The broader the category, the more clearly the wave impressions are outlined. The wave pattern of the comprehensible stock price averages – such as the Dow-Jones, *The New York Times*, or Standard Statistics averages – will correctly reflect the cyclical position of the market as a whole. Therefore, purchases and sales of a diversified list of representative stocks in accordance with the movements of the averages will result in profits, as their aggregate market value will swing in sympathy with the general market. But for the seeker of maximum profits consistent with safety, it is not enough to buy or sell a group of stocks without separate analysis of each individual stock. These individual studies may reveal that some companies are experiencing a cycle differing greatly from that of the market as a whole. A prominent example was the case of American Can in the spring of 1935.

The accompanying charts depict the analysis of American Can by The Wave Principle. In Figure 21 the complete monthly range history is shown from June, 1932 – the beginning of the bull movement – to June, 1935, the time when the "orthodox top" occurred. The action of the stock from that point on to completion of the cyclical correction in December, 1937, is shown in "trend lines." This monthly record condenses the weekly and daily details into the five broad Primary waves that complete a cyclical movement. These relatively broad charts also help materially in maintaining the proper perspective.

FIGURES 21, 22, 23 & 24

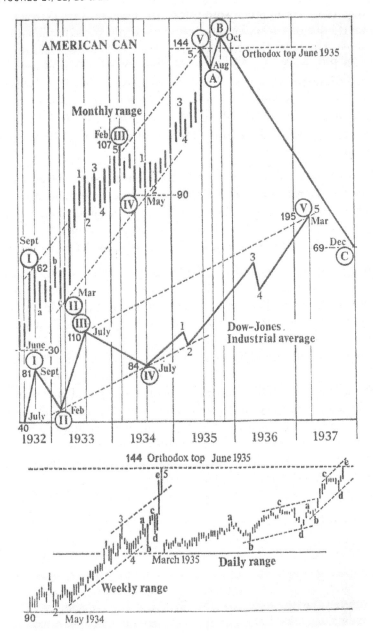

When the important Fifth Primary Wave of the cycle commenced in May, 1931 – or in other words, when the Primary Wave IV reaction was completed – it became necessary to study the market action more closely. Hence Figure 22, which shows the weekly price record of the Fifth Primary Wave. And after this Primary Wave had progressed through Intermediate Wave 4, it became important to follow the daily price ranges, as shown in Figure 23. The Fifth Intermediate Wave started in March, 1935; and five Minor waves were completed by June, 1935. This signalled the "orthodox top" of the main bull movement in American Can at 144.

Following the "orthodox top" of the bull cycle in American Can, there developed a reaction to 136-137 in August 1935 – forming Wave A. Then a rally to 149-150 In October 1935 – forming Wave B, the irregular but final top. From this point developed the long Wave C, in five intermediate movements, terminating at 69 in December, 1937.

At the time of the "orthodox top" in American Can, the investor would have observed the striking difference between the cyclical positions of that stock and of the general market. See Figure 24, which outlines the trend lines of the important Primary Waves of the Dow-Jones Industrial Averages. In March, 1935, American Can was in the final stages of a bull cycle (Fifth Intermediate Wave of the Fifth Primary). On the other hand the general market was just commencing the Fifth Primary Wave, and still had to experience the five upward Intermediate Waves. By June 1935, the long term investor in American Can would have realized (1) that any further appreciation in that stock would be highly uncertain; and (2) that much greater profits were available in the general market with minimum risks. From that point the general market advanced nearly 80 points or 65 per cent.

Bibliography

Appel, James. *Winning Systems in the Stock Market.* (Capitalist Reporter; New York, 1974.)

Bolton, A. Hamilton. *A Critical Appraisal of the Elliott Wave Principle.* (The Bank Credit Analyst; Toronto, 1960.)

Bretz, John. *Juncture Recognition in the Stock Market.* (Vantage Press; New York, 1964.)

Clemence, Richard V., and Doody, Francis C. *The Schumpeterian System.* (Kelly; New York, 1956.)

Cogan, Peter L. *The Rhythmic Cycles of Optimism and Pessimism.* (William Frederick; New York, 1968.)

Dewey, Edward R. *Cycles.* (Foundation for the Study of Cycles; Pittsburgh, 1974.)

Drew, Garfield. *New Methods for Profit in the Stock Market.* (Pitman; New York, 1954.)

Elliott, R. N. *The Wave Principle.* (Elliott, 1938.)

Elliott, R. N. *Nature's Law.* (Elliott, 1946.)

Elliott Wave Course (The). (Investors Educators; Chicago, 1962.)

Flumiani, C. M. *The Reconstruction of the Elliott Wave Principle.* (Stock Market Chartist Club of America; Wibraham, Mass., 1970.)

Fraser, Ian. *The Elliott Wave Principle.* (Article included in *The Encyclopedia of Stock Market Techniques.* Investors Intelligence; Larchmont, N.Y., 1962.)

Gann, W. D. *Truth of the Stock Tape.* (Financial Guardian; New York, 1932.)

Garrett, William C. *Investing for Profit with Torque Analysis of Stock Market Cycles.* (Prentice Hall; New Jersey, 1972.)

Gelderen, J. van. Springvloed; Beschouwing Over Industriele Ontwikkeling en Prijsbeweging (c. 1920.)

Greiner, P. P. and Whitcomb, H. C. *The Dow Theory and the 70-Year Forecast Record.* (Investors Intelligence; Larchmont, N.Y., 1961.)

Hambridge, Jay. Practical Application of Dynamic Symmetry: The Law of Phyllotaxis. (Yale, 1920.)

Jiler, William, L. *How Charts can Help You in the Stock Market.* (Commodity Research; New York, 1962.)

King, J. L. *Human Behaviour and Wall Street.* (Swallow Press; Chicago, 1974.)

Klein, F. C and Prestbo, J. A. *News and the Market.* (Regner; Chicago, 1974.)

Kondratieff, N. P. Die langen Wellen de Konjunktur. (1928.)

Krow, Harvey A., *Stock Market Behaviour.* (Random House; New York, 1969.)

Merrill, Arthur. *Behaviour of Prices on Wall Street.* (Analysis Press; Chappaqua, 1966.)

Notley, Ian S. *Market Trend Analysis.* (Draper Dobie; Toronto, 1976.)

Notley, Ian S. *Market Trend Analysis Practical.* (Draper Dobie; Toronto, 1976.)

O'Connor, William. *Stocks, Wheat and Pharaohs.* (Wener Books; New York, 1961.)

Scheineman, William K. *Why Most Investors are Mostly Wrong Most of the Time.* (Weybright and Talley; New York, 1960.)

Schillinger, J. The Mathematical Basis of the Arts. (1956.)

Schultz, John. *The Intelligent Chartist.* (Trend and Value; New York, 1962.)

Schuman, James B., and Rosenau, David, *The Kondratieff Wave*. (World Publishing; New York, 1974.)

Schumpeter, J. *Theory of Economic Development*. (Harvard U.P., Cambridge, Mass., 1934.)

Supplement to the Bank Credit Analyst. 1961, 1962 and addendum, 1963, 1965, 1966, 1967, 1968. Contributors: A. Hamilton Bolton, A. J. Frost, Russell L. Hall, Walter E. White, et al. (The Bank Credit Analyst Ltd., Bermuda.)

Tompkins, Peter. *Secrets of the Great Pyramid*.

FREE EBOOK VERSION

As a buyer of the print book of Supertiming you can now download the eBook version free of charge to read on an eBook reader, your smartphone or your computer. Simply go to:

http://ebooks.harriman-house.com/supertiming

or point your smartphone at the QRC below.

COMPLETE YOUR HARRIMAN
HOUSE TRADING LIBRARY

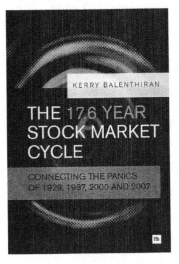

The 17.6 Year Stock Market Cycle

Connecting the Panics of 1929, 1987, 2000 and 2007

By Kerry Balenthiran

"The 17.6 Year Stock Market Cycle provides an additional piece of ammunition for traders as they approach the market."

Traders' Magazine

Available as paperback and eBook

Crowd Money

A Practical Guide to Macro Behavioural Technical Analysis

By Eoin Treacy

"Fuller and Treacy's approach reveals something astonishing taking place in the markets right now."

Traders' Magazine

Available as paperback and eBook

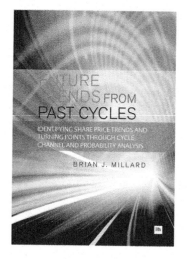

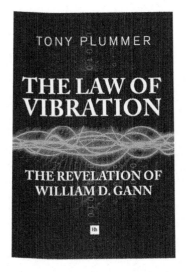

The Law of Vibration

The revelation of William D. Gann

By Tony Plummer

"Tony Plummer introduces us to an underlying order, not just in the stock market, but in the universe as an entirety."

Available as paperback and eBook

Mastering Hurst

A modern treatment of Hurst's original system of financial market analysis

By Christopher Grafton

"A carefully constructed, thorough and extremely readable guide to a complicated area of technical analysis."

Money Maker Magazine

Available as paperback and eBook

*All print books except *The Definitive Guide to Point and Figure* come with a free eBook edition. See our website or contact us for details.

CPSIA information can be obtained
at www.ICGtesting.com
Printed in the USA
BVOW08s0545051217
501912BV00018B/1284/P